Praise

"Dr. Milke points out that both the Klein and Notley governments faced the challenges of a weak energy sector and provincial finances crippled by years of deficit spending. Both faced the temptation to pursue interventionist policies in the energy sector, and both faced the challenge of inexorable growth in the health and educations sectors. Both even had a special interest in beer.... The NDP government needlessly interjected itself there; Klein (who always enjoyed a pint or two) simply privatized it."

—**Preston Manning,** founder of the federal Reform Party and Canadian Alliance, and former Leader of the Official Opposition in the Parliament of Canada.

"In this well-researched, entertaining read, Mark Milke takes readers on a journey over the last 30 years that creates such a stark contrast between the two Alberta premiers that it makes Ralph Klein's accomplishments of the early 1990s look even more herculean with each passing year. After reading *Ralph vs. Rachel,* you may long for the days of balanced budgets, flat taxes, and, yes, even Ralph-bucks."

—**Scott Hennig**, Vice President, Canadian Taxpayers Federation

"Mark Milke's tale of two premiers is a masterful lesson on how two different Alberta premiers dealt with similar challenges with dramatically different approaches. The premier that took the path of trust in Albertans helped to unleash many years of unparalleled growth of the Alberta economy. The other produced unparalleled bloat in government and government debt.

While Mark paints on the Alberta canvas, the landscape for his ideas—and the cogent explanation of them—is universal. Mark Milke examines the ideas, slogans, and policies of many who call themselves progressives and deconstructs them to help us understand why good intentions are never good enough."

—**Charles Adler**, Host of Corus Entertainment's Charles Adler Tonight

About the author

Mark Milke is a public policy analyst, keynote speaker, author and columnist with five books and dozens of studies published across Canada and internationally in the last two decades. Mark's work has been published by think tanks in Canada, the United States and Europe including the Fraser Institute, the American Enterprise Institute and Brussels-based Centre for European Studies. His columns have appeared in the *Globe and Mail, National Post* and *Maclean's*.

Mark is president of the Sir Winston Churchill Society of Calgary and a past President of Civitas—a Society for Ideas. His doctoral dissertation in International Relations and Political Philosophy analyzed the rhetoric of anti-Americanism in Canada while his Master's thesis chronicled the double standard on human rights in East Asia. Mark lives in Calgary and is an active hiker, skier and runner with an interest in architecture, photography, cities, and history. His website is www.markmilke.com

Published by Thomas & Black

ISBN: 978-0-9687915-5-4

Photos used on cover:
"Alberta Premier Ralph Klein Giving Speech in Calgary Alberta", Photo by Chuck Szmurlo is licensed under CC BY 2.0

"Rachel Notley", Photo by: Connor Mah is licensed under CC BY 2.0

Cartoons from Malcolm Mayes and John Larter reproduced with permission from Artizans.com.

Printed in Canada

Book distribution by Sandhill Book Marketing
www.sandhillbooks.com

From *Ralph vs. Rachel*

On NDP tax policies

"If a common link exists in both military failures, it is the obsession by those in command to stick to some existing notion at all costs. Napoleon wanted Tsar Alexander I to sign a peace treaty that would have eliminated English trade with Russia; Charles d'Albret allowed himself to be drawn into battle when he should have backed away and allowed the English to advance to the coast and Calais. Which is where we might consider another not-so-magnificent obsession, and a hill New Democrats apparently wish to defend: their decades-long belief that Albertans are dramatically undertaxed."

The 1990s Rorschach test

"Health care and education, and the Klein government's temporary reduction in spending in both ministries was, and still is, like a Rorschach test for Albertans. Many people see what they see and cannot envision any other image."

Your heroes explain you

"The Notley-Guevara, Loyola-Chavez sympathies are notable, not because one expects the premier or Loyola, who chairs the standing committee on resource stewardship, to one day hire Latin American revolutionaries to run Alberta's prisons or to nationalize Alberta's energy sector, though, in the 2014 leadership race, Loyola did like the idea of 60-per-cent royalty rates. The sympathies matter because, whether Guevara or Chavez, New Democrats still seemed impressed by revolutionary rhetoric over the hard-work reality of how economies, actual justice, and countries are built and prosper."

Also by Mark Milke

Tax Me I'm Canadian

Stealth Confiscation

A Nation of Serfs?

Barbarians in the Garden City

RALPH
VS.
RACHEL

A TALE OF TWO ALBERTA PREMIERS

Mark Milke

Foreword by Preston Manning

Thomas & Black

Contents

Foreword by Mr. Preston Manning

"He's doing what he said he'd do."

Ralph Klein's chief of staff, Rod Love, in 1993

Abraham Lincoln once said, "The past is the cause of the present and the present is the cause of the future." Thus, in Alberta, the policies and practices of past governments have significantly affected the current state of the province, and the policies and practices of the current government will significantly affect our future.

Alberta's first provincial government—its one and only Liberal government—distinguished itself by amassing a large public debt, which two subsequent provincial governments struggled to reduce. When the Depression hit, Alberta was forced to default on the principal of that debt—the only province to do so—and was unable to borrow again until the early 1950s. It was the government of my father, Ernest C. Manning—operating on a "pay as you go" policy and blessed with petroleum revenues after the Leduc discovery—that committed the province to budget balancing and a policy of successful debt retirement rather than debt accumulation.

But now, fast forward to the present. How the finances and economy of the province are managed is again a major issue and one very much affecting our future. In this book, Dr. Mark Milke has rendered a valuable service by chronicling two fundamentally different approaches to the governance of Alberta's finances and economy—that pursued by the late conservative Premier Ralph Klein and that currently being pursued by NDP Premier Rachel Notley.

The first chapter in the book is titled "Early NDP temptations," and I am in general agreement with his assessment that the supposedly conservative governments of Ed Stelmach and Alison Redford strayed a long way from conservative values and principles, thus paving the way for the election of an NDP government.

Dr. Milke points out that both the Klein and Notley governments faced the challenges of a weak energy sector and provincial finances crippled by years of deficit spending. Both faced the temptation to pursue interventionist policies in the energy sector, and both faced the challenge of inexorable growth in the health and educations sectors. Both even had a special interest in beer.

But there the similarities end.

Whereas the current NDP government continues to pile up deficits and debt, Klein pursued budget balancing and sought to cut taxes.

Whereas the current NDP government pursues spasmodic and unpredictable intervention in the energy sector, Klein sought to create stability and a favourable climate for energy-industry investment and growth.

Whereas the current NDP government criticizes previous Conservative governments in Alberta for "squandering" resource revenues (but has not itself deposited a nickel into the province's rainy-day funds), Klein deposited $20 billion into the province's three resource funds, including the Heritage Fund.

And with respect to the retail sector for beer, whereas the NDP government has even needlessly interjected itself there, Klein (who always enjoyed a pint or two) simply privatized it.

It was Thomas Jefferson who once wrote, "I can think of no safer depository for the ultimate powers of society, than the people themselves." And, anticipating the objection, very prevalent today from our media and political elites, that "the people themselves" are not to be trusted to exercise such powers responsibly, he added, "And if you think them (the people) not fit to exercise control with a wholesome discretion, the remedy is not to take it from them, but to *inform their discretion*."

In *Ralph vs. Rachel*, Dr. Mark Milke seeks to "inform our discretion." I highly commend it to your attention.

Preston Manning PC CC AOE
Calgary
September, 2018

Preston Manning is a life-long Albertan, son of Alberta's longest-serving premier, Ernest C. Manning. He is the founder of the federal Reform Party and Canadian Alliance, forerunners to the Conservative Party of Canada, and served as leader of the Official Opposition in the Parliament of Canada.

RALPH
PROSPERITY CHEQUES
YOU HEARD ME... THE PREMIER'S ALREADY SOLVED THE DISTRIBUTION PROBLEM!
MAYES edmonton journal
artizans.com

Introduction: Ralph's World

"Ralph is the only politician I know where individuals still come up to me on the street and want to tell me about the time they hung out with him."

Calgary Sun Columnist Rick Bell, in 2018

Two Alberta premiers, two approaches

A few years back, I gave a speech to the Canadian Well Logging Society, which is not as its name might suggest—about wells or logging, at least not the water and wood variety. They are instead composed mainly of petrophysicists and engineers, the folk on the front lines of oil exploration in Alberta. When the economy is healthy, they perform and analyze the initial field measurements of wells to uncover the earth's secrets; does this hoped-for deposit actually contain oil, or will the company drill a multi-million dollar dry well?

When the economy is poor, as it was in the spring of 2016 when I spoke to the group, they are among the first, highly educated Albertans to face unemployment. After my speech where I laid out the "macro" problem—tens of billions of investment dollars that vaporized after the 2014 oil price crash—I then heard the personal stories that came in the wake of that collapse. One fellow, a dad, moved from Venezuela seven years previous to escape the anti-reality economics of the Hugo Chavez regime; he recently lost his engineering job in Calgary. To put food on his family's table, he was working at a shop that repaired bicycles. Another member told me that she finally found work at a casino on a First Nations reserve. This university-educated woman, who once made six figures-plus in the energy sector, was now serving up cocktails and beer, for a sixth of her previous salary. Both types of work are valuable in their own right but not what either person trained for. That night, the president of the association told me that unemployment among her members was 50 per cent.

If I told those stories to Premier Rachel Notley, I think she would be empathetic. I don't know the premier but a friend who does and is her neighbour in Edmonton tells me that Rachel Notley is down-to-earth, grounded, real. And she has demonstrated that vis-à-vis those who are not. After federal NDP Leader Jagmeet Singh criticized the Saudi Arabian regime and its treatment of women, and yet refused to endorse Alberta oil as a replacement—Singh is opposed to pipelines and Alberta's oil sands—the Alberta premier ripped into her federal party leader. Notley said she was from the wing of the NDP that understands "you don't bring about equality and fairness without focusing on jobs for regular working people."

If Ralph Klein were alive, he too would sympathize with those hit by the recent Alberta downturn. When I first moved to Calgary, I heard a story—possibly apocryphal but it sounds like the late premier—about Klein, dating back to his time as mayor in the early 1980s. Apparently a woman having trouble paying her power bill was informed by the city utility that her electricity was soon to be shut off if payment was not received immediately. This was the early 1980s and unemployment was in the double digits. After the constituent managed to tell Klein about her plight, some bureaucrat somewhere in the annals of bureaucracy was summoned, received an earful, and the city-owned utility suddenly worked out a longer repayment schedule. The story, which I could never confirm, matters, because many such anecdotes that have arisen over the decades and were verified, all revealed a fellow who understood "average" Albertans because he was one and never forgot it.

Imperfections

The stories about Klein and the approach to Singh from Notley reveal something, and not because one must agree with either politician on their every decision or expect perfection, personally or policy-wise. As with the rest of humanity—the rest of us—neither Klein nor Notley have been flawless. Klein was once famously drunk at the wrong time, evening, and place—the premier threw money at a homeless fellow in a shelter, just before Christmas. *Ouch*. Notley, in giving advice on how to mitigate the impact of her carbon tax, once advised Albertans to take public transit, bike, and walk more often. As described later in this book, that was a "tell," and a bit hectoring. But neither Klein's drunken episode nor Notley's sober comments mean either lacked compassion for ordinary people. In both cases, I would assume the opposite, actually, and chalk it up to the drink in one case and a stumble in the other.

But it does beg the question because politics is about what

governments do and not just personalities: How should Albertans think about each premier? And how should we judge them?

Answer: By results.

Since 1993 and more recently, Albertans have been given a case study in two diverse approaches to the role of government, taxes, regulation, and much more. Look even closer, and see two unique views of human nature and how the world works. To get to the results but also the "why" of developments in recent years—how "Klein's World" turned into "Notley Nation" (as two authors of a book on the premier characterized the latter development)—I start with what amounts to a detour: the province's almost-first NDP government. That was not Notley's, but arguably the late-era Progressive Conservatives who increasingly embraced the language and policies of the party that upended them in 2015. The ebb and flow of politics often washes politicians onto shores they never planned for, but some of the rhetoric and policies in the late PC era already set their ship's rudder—and Alberta—to such a destination. The late-era PCs were weirdly reminiscent in words and policy to a government in British Columbia, in the 1990s, one in which Rachel Notley worked.

The book then plunges into the Alberta NDP's reign. It includes a decades-long belief that if only Albertans would tax themselves more, all would be well, or at least balanced. I also compare the economic tempests endured by both premiers upon arriving in office and then their distinct choices, beliefs, temptations, and paths. Next, comparisons are given based on each premier's first three years in office—everything from jobs, taxes, and Heritage Fund deposits to whether flat taxes were a wild and crazy idea or more progressive than thought (I side with the latter view).

In all that, the occasional myth-busting chapter is thrown in: Ralph Klein's government saved health care and education. To not grasp that is to engage in magical thinking. I then remind the rest of Canada that they were lucky Alberta existed in the Klein years; the giant sucking sound during his time in office was that of the province's job creation machine drawing in the unemployed from St. John's to Surrey. Alberta's opportunity culture was a boon to all, from the highly educated to those who never finished high school. It would be helpful if that reality was more widely recognized, country-wide, today.

Some still think Alberta's past prosperity arrived by accident. In the last chapter, that myth is subject to data detonation. But I do offer up a caveat: Even the so-called luckiest places on the planet can crash their economies due to political choices. It happened to entire countries in the past. It is happening now to Alberta, and care of anti-energy and anti-Alberta attacks financed by those who think Canadians should do all the heavy lifting on carbon reductions—this while China builds hundreds of new coal plants. Moderation in policy is a virtue, and Canadians could use more of it in Edmonton, Ottawa, and Victoria, but also from those engaged in economy-wrecking Canada's first-world energy model of responsibility and opportunity.

If there is a theme in Ralph vs. Rachel beyond the comparisons for the curious, it is that opportunity matters. My background is not one of privilege, and I well remember my parents' own difficult struggle to pay bills and provide for us kids (I have three siblings). In the early 1980s, the British Columbia economy collapsed and, with it, everything my parents owned. The only home I'd known since birth, in Kelowna, and the one my dad built before I was born, was soon lost to the bank, forever. My Mom and Dad started over, with Mom serving customers and cleaning tables to pay the rent. Mom, always social, enjoyed the work with others at the Sears cafeteria in Kelowna; it didn't make the loss any easier.

Which brings me back to out-of-work engineers, or a cleaner, Helen, who once worked in an office building where I had a desk. I love Alberta for its soaring Rocky Mountain peaks and other natural wonders but also for its entrepreneurial can-do spirit and people. When the 2014 downturn hit and created a 30-per-cent glut in the downtown office market, Helen came to mind, as did others engaged in similar work. Helen was exactly who I feared for when the economy turned south—the cleaners, restaurant servers, guys on rigs, and others in support service who are laid off first and often hit the hardest. While not much could be done about a collapse in the oil price in 2014, the critical choice for politicians is to not make a bad situation worse through ill-advised policies based on whims, ideologies, or passions that then further hamper the flourishing Alberta everyone needs back. The choices politicians make do matter, and this book is about past and present choices, the results, and the opportunities still needed for all.

Mark Milke
Calgary, Alberta
September 2018

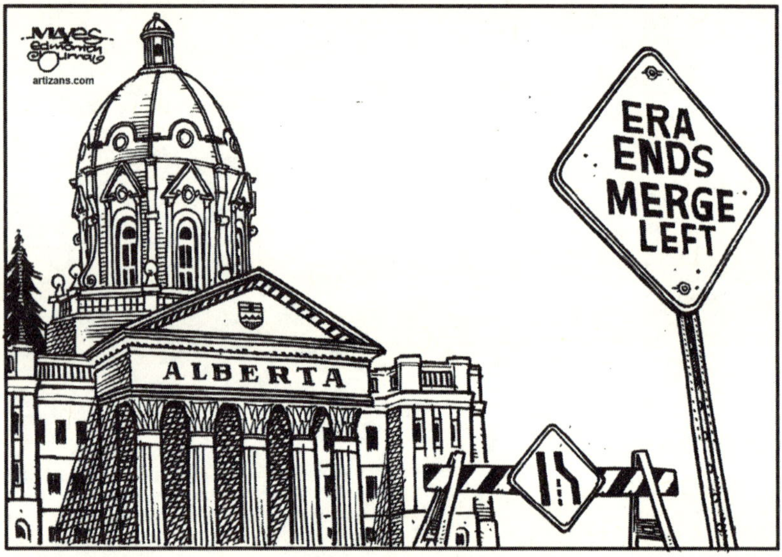
artizans.com
ALBERTA
ERA
ENDS
MERGE
LEFT

1

Early NDP temptations: The late PC age, circa 2006–2015

"Never again will this government or the people of this province have to set aside another tax dollar on debt.... Those days are over and they're over for good, as far as my government is concerned...."

Ralph Klein, 2004, announcing Alberta was debt-free[1]

"We have seen for the last 15 years in this province, what I think is a parochial debate, about words like debt and deficit."

Alison Redford, premier 2011–2014[2]

Fair-share rhetoric from Progressive Conservatives

When Alberta's Progressive Conservative politicians first used the phrase "fair share" in the mid-2000s, I had an out-of-province experience: I thought I was in British Columbia, a decade previous, when the New Democrats ran the province and the chief ideological interventionist, Glen Clark, was the NDP finance minister. Back then, Premier Mike Harcourt and Clark (who later became premier, in 1996) went after businesses and taxpayers with new and higher imposts.

They also tied up the forestry and mining sectors in regulations that only a Chilean could love—the latter benefitted from the exodus of investment from British Columbia into South America.

And British Columbia's New Democrats loved "fairness" language. After gaining power in 1991, they tripped over each other to repeat "fair" in defending $1.5 billion in tax hikes in two budgets. "It is not fun to tax the rich," said then NDP minister of agriculture, Corky Evans, "it is only fair."[3] Education Minister Moe Sihota called the new taxes "tough, but fair."[4] And Ujjal Dosanjh, the NDP premier at the end, just before his party imploded in the 2001 election, argued that "a great budget is for ensuring that the top eight percent of all income earners in B.C. pay their fair share of taxes—for a change."[5]

Such language and policies were expected from New Democrats, whether in British Columbia, federally, or in Saskatchewan—where an abundance of such rhetoric and policy and no warm-weather charms to compensate—stalled the latter province's population growth for four decades. Or even in British Columbia, where the NDP over ten years managed two feats no other government had ever done: to turn British Columbia into a have-not province and send interprovincial migration negative, and east, to Ralph Klein's Alberta. This happened in a decade when the rest of Canada and much of the world was booming.

Fairness language enacted into policy leads to such outcomes. With the NDP's ideology anchored in faulty fixed-pie economic conceptions concocted by a 19th-century German philosopher, additionally influenced by 1930s Fabian socialism, and the 1970s Waffle Manifesto, New Democratic Party politicians and its activist network long looked at prosperity as static and conceived of new ways to cut it up. They rarely understood, or cared, about another more positive option: free people up to flourish. For political practitioners with a reflex to intervention, the preference is to perch and be ready to pounce on success, ever-ready to demand that an ever-larger "fair share" of our labour, of our income, of our life's work, be sent upwards to politicians to spend.

The f-word in Wild Rose Country

Which brings us back to Alberta politicians from a half-named conservative party in the middle part of the last decade and their conversion to the rhetoric of redistribution. In 2006, a cadre of leadership contenders vied for the Progressive Conservative Party's leadership in the wake of Premier Ralph Klein's resignation. Almost all endorsed the notion that Albertans deserved more from Alberta's main wealth-creating engine, the oil and gas companies, both big and small. The candidates' language was ripped straight from decades-old NDP platforms about "fairness."

Thus, Edmonton MLA and former economic development minister, Mark Norris, observed in June 2006 that "the average guy sees all this vast development going on and wonders if we're getting a fair share."[6] (He later characterized the conventional royalties as fine but thought that oil sands companies were problematic.[7]) Ted Morton, the conservative University of Calgary political science professor-turned-candidate also mused about a possible hike in royalties. "I know the companies would squawk," said Morton, as he outlined a justification for a higher take from the energy sector. "But the fact is they need the infrastructure as badly as the communities and workers do."[8] Dave Hancock, a onetime advanced education minister, was in favour of the new fairness lingo. He asserted that "changing industry circumstances" required a comprehensive review. Former intergovernmental affairs minister Ed Stelmach remarked that he would "not rule out revisiting the whole royalty rate structure." As with many politicians, Stelmach spoke in the collective "we," common to Canada's left-wing parties. "The raw resources belong to Albertans," remarked Stelmach. "Once we sell them, they're gone. It's critical we get the best return on them today." Jim Dinning, the finance minister under Ralph Klein between 1993 and 1997, noted public discontent with the royalty rates: "People ask, 'Are we getting our fair share?'"[9]

The NDP-style rhetoric intensified throughout the PC leadership contest. At a September 2006 leadership debate, Alanna Delong said, "We need to make sure we're getting the best possible value out of these resources." With reference to what was then considered a high price for oil ($60 per barrel), Dave Hancock warmed to the idea of higher royalties on the industry: "We're in a new environment," he remarked, adding, "It would seem to make sense that the incentive structure should be changed." Hancock was not hinting at a reduction. Another candidate, Gary McPherson, argued the existing structure was "one-sided," while Ted Morton looked at the present investment boom and thought it demanded higher royalties: "The world is beating down the door to get a piece of the oil sands. It certainly seems to me that we could and should get a better return for Albertans." Dinning again used the two words long associated with Canada's left: "The government has got to help Albertans be confident they're getting a fair share of the resources they own."[10]

In theory, there was nothing wrong with revisiting royalty rates, or asking the question. Resource rents are like any other rent. Set the price too high and you lose tenants. Set the price too low and the owner foregoes market rent. Even the provincial department of energy believed that the province could collect an extra $1 billion in royalties without harming the energy sector.[11] The problem with the 2006 chatter was not the question; it was in the rhetoric that mimicked the class warfare language of the Canadian left, and, in particular, the policy and politics of the New Democratic Party.

For example, in its 2004 election manifesto, the Alberta NDP under Brian Mason pledged to "scrap the Royalty Tax Credit for oil sands companies" and wanted to "scale back other royalty reduction programs"—whatever those might be. The NDP also demanded "a royalty windfall surcharge on oil when prices exceeded $25 a barrel and on natural gas if prices topped $4 per gigajoule."[12] Given that oil had mostly been higher than 25 dollars since 1999[13] and natural gas regularly exceeded four dollars since 2002,[14] the 2004 NDP platform, if enacted, would have added extra tax to every barrel of oil and every gigajoule of gas. That would hit consumers and exporters with the new and higher made-in-Alberta taxes on its primary sector. The NDP's 2004 plan was akin to an Ontario government applying newer and higher taxes on the production of automobiles in Ontario—on any vehicle above $25,000—or Saskatchewan suggesting a wheat export tax. But much of what the NDP wished for in 2004 was rhetorically endorsed in 2006 by the leading candidates for the Progressive Conservative Party's top job. It begged the question, far into the future: Why not elect the real thing?

A few voices battled the unproven assumption that the existing royalty regime was "unfair." Lyle Oberg, a health minister before resigning to run in the 2006 leadership contest, pointed out the "real danger" in messing with a "good, justifiable revenue-sharing formula [the province has] now." He noted that after tens of billions of dollars were invested annually, dramatic changes tended to make capital markets "very skittish." Oberg was a seer without knowing it when he predicted: "If you show any signs of sudden changes, that market will vanish."[15] Greg Melchin, Alberta's energy minister during the leadership campaign, said "Yes, energy prices are going up, but we're a high-cost producer and our costs are going up, too." He reminded the candidates, public, and media to "be aware of long-term concerns of capital. You've got to be part of a stable, dependable and predictable fiscal regime."[16]

By late November 2006, just days before the leadership vote, the topic again captured the candidates' attention. Morton and Dinning, either a likely replacement for Klein based on delegates and organization, both again referenced royalties near the end. Morton accused Dinning of having been a latecomer to the issue, "but I think he's caught up with me." In response, Dinning exercised some late-game caution: "I'm not prepared to play fast and loose with [oil sands] investment," he replied, adding that "To deliver that kind of message to the investment sector sends a cold ripple of angst." Ed Stelmach also now played coy, acknowledging public discontent but characterizing any decision on raised royalty rates as a mere hypothetical. "They're just asking if it's fair or not," he said of public attitudes.[17]

Enter the new premier

It was unlikely any of the 2006-era Progressive Conservative candidates intentionally meant to recast themselves as Saskatchewan's post-1930s chase-capital-away Prairie ideologues. Nor did they likely intend to replicate policies from B.C.'s 1990s-era New Democrats who never met an entrepreneur, business, or entire sector they could not crater with taxes and regulation as thick as a rose bush. (A joke in British Columbia at the time: How does the NDP encourage more small business? Answer: Tax and regulate big businesses until they shrink.) Nor would Morton, Dinning, et al. consciously imitate the third-place entity in the Alberta legislature, the New Democratic Party, led by bus-driver Brian Mason.

Also, Jim Dinning and Ted Morton were anything but interventionists. Their words and actions on other matters reflected a realistic, small-c conservative view of how government should be run. Dinning was a 1990s-era co-architect with Klein of the reformed government, responsible for many of the budget reforms, be it transparent budget assumptions, accountability legislation, ending subsidies to business, and privatization efforts. Without Dinning's early, disciplined prudence as finance minister, later tax relief introduced under the next minister of finance, Stockwell Day, would have been truncated, if available at all. Dinning was at the core of the most sensible government in Alberta in decades.

Likewise, Ted Morton was no shrinking red violet. Outside of government and in it, Morton charted a prudent course. (Later in government Morton opposed the billions of taxpayer dollars risked by the Ed Stelmach government on the private North West refinery; he was also the cabinet minister who pushed the Progressive Conservatives to move to a balanced budget—a plan then thwarted by the premier. Morton, we should recall, was about to quit as finance minister on principle in January 2011, rather than let the premier delay a return to black ink beyond the 2012 budget year; Stelmach's already-announced position broke a promise that Stelmach, Morton, and the other PCs had made to Albertans. Before Morton could quit, Stelmach saw the writing on the political wall, and himself resigned as premier.)

Nonetheless, in 2006 the Progressive Conservative rhetoric was soon to be entrenched in the premier's office by Ed Stelmach. Stelmach was in pre-law in 1973, when family priorities led him to abandon that trajectory and instead take over the family farm. A onetime reeve, he jumped into provincial politics in 1993 to help Alberta's Conservatives pare back the size of government. As his own campaign website described it, Stelmach was "inspired by the deficit cutting agenda" of Ralph Klein. After his election that year as an MLA, he was part of the post-1993 backbench group of fiscal hawks known as the "Deep Six," who pushed Klein and the rest of their caucus to cut government spending. From Ukrainian stock and widely praised as honest and nice, the 54-year-old farmer came up the middle between Morton and Dinning in the early December 2006 leadership contest.

But 1993 was a political lifetime away, and with growth pressure in every nook, cranny, and suburb of Alberta, the province wanted even more resource money to pay for services and infrastructure. After becoming Alberta's 13th premier, Stelmach commissioned a royalty review. Perhaps predictably, given the leadership campaign theme, the Alberta Royalty Review Panel also evoked redistributionist language, as opposed to more neutral business phrasing that one might expect from an impartial analysis. When the panel's work was concluded and the *Our Fair Share* report released in September 2007, its members bluntly concluded that "Albertans do not receive their fair share from energy development." Their report called for

$2 billion in extra royalties, one-seventh of the $14-billion-plus in resource revenues that the province was forecast to receive that budget year. One month later, the premier appeared on TV to explain his final decision on the panel's recommendations. He again used the language of the left: The report, he said, "delivers the fair share Albertans rightly expect."[18] The next day the premier hit the oil and gas sector with $1.5 billion in royalty increases.

The Stelmach decision was immediately attacked from both sides. George Gosbee, president of Tristone, an investment firm in Calgary, predicted the royalty hit would "result in the loss of the winter drilling season, a decrease in royalties for 2008 and 2009, and in a nutshell, it will not be a bigger pie. It will be a smaller pie." He told investors on a conference call that he was "in utter shock."[19] The Canadian Association of Oilwell Drilling Contractors also chimed in, predicting 30,000 lost jobs. "The winter season is toast,"[20] said Don Herring. On the other side, NDP Leader Brian Mason slammed Stelmach, saying he failed to "stand up for Albertans" when the premier neglected to adopt every single recommendation in the royalty report. Opposition leader Kevin Taft, a perennial critic of the Klein government and of oil and gas in general since his days in academia, said the government failed by accepting a half-loaf. Taft wanted more and not less in royalties.[21] If Stelmach thought he walked a moderate path, he instead put himself in the middle of a highway with vehicles speeding past him that clipped him from the left and right. Ironically, the premier, who thought he was standing up to big oil, had it backwards: FirstEnergy Capital, another Calgary-based investment firm, summarized the Stelmach royalty framework as: "Big Oil wins, Little Oil loses."[22] Over the next year, the report's recommendations and the government's new royalty framework would be eviscerated and reworked piece by piece. Stelmach's rhetoric had done little other than raise expectations among the public, botch the details, and anger supporters, critics, and fair-minded observers alike. And the experiment entrenched the language of entitlement and redistribution in the Premier's office.

Health care: We're all New Democrats now

The royalty fiasco and the language were not the only bits of evidence that the PC Party had lost any touch with free-enterprise conservatism and were busily tacking to an interventionist left. Another signal came with the next leadership contest in 2011.[23] Similar to the 2006 run, except relative to the health-care issue, original thinking that *might* involve scouring the world for best practices was off the table. Instead, multiple leadership contenders again channeled historic New Democratic Party clichés from everyone from Tommy Douglas to Jack Layton. Thus, when Progressive Conservative leadership candidate Gary Mar suggested opening Alberta's health-care sector to some private options (and sensibly, in the context of continued universality), fellow leadership contenders launched a disinformation *blitzkrieg*. Calgary lawyer Alison Redford expressed "surprise" and argued the real issue is equality: "I don't believe Albertans want us to have a system that can create preferential treatment." Edmonton businessman and MLA, Doug Horner, whose family had a long history of public service, chimed in against more private options because "We've got lots to do in our publicly funded system."

The 2011 leadership candidates were also parroting NDP allies, such as public-sector unions heavily intertwined in government-run health care, and increasingly influential in the PC Party and government post-2006. The Alberta Union of Provincial Employees asserted, against all international evidence and domestic realities such as long wait times, that "our public health-care system works." Then there was the usual cliché charge that health care was somehow exempt from dollars-and-cents realities. Bev Dick, vice president of the Alberta union that represents nurses, argued Mar was wrong to view health care as a "commodity."

Facts and Mar aside, the PC leadership rhetoric not only followed the NDP and their allies' lead but was disingenuous. Redford's "preferential treatment" comment referenced the possibility that the wealthy might find ways to obtain treatment faster than sitting in the health-care lineups endemic in the Canadian health-care system. But Redford well knew that many executives and others in her circle regularly flew to the United States to buy medical treatment. Their flights were not the problem; it was how health-care queues for the rest of us made a mockery of the claim that Canadian health care was universal—except it wasn't, not if outcomes and queues were measured.

On the health-care-is-not-a-commodity assertion, nurses, doctors, and receptionists all needed to be paid for their labour; medical companies had to pay someone to manufacture medical equipment, and researchers do not work on new drugs for free. Labour, products, and equipment were indeed commodities. Even the nurses' union would use the language of markets in its bargaining, pointing to the "demand" for nurses as high and that if wages and benefits were not competitive, the "supply" of nurses could go elsewhere. During 2007 contract negotiations, when hourly increases of 15 to 27 per cent were on the table, the director of labour relations for the United Nurses of Alberta remarked that the provincial offer was "a competitive agreement" but questioned whether it was "enough to deal with the nursing shortage."[24] In other words, the labour of nurses was subject to marketplace dynamics. The province was encouraged by the union to pay more, lest the supply of such professionals dry up.

Rather than endorse a magical, cost-free, fairy-tale approach to health care, the other 2011 leadership candidates should have leapt to Mar's defence. Instead they offered up straw-men arguments (Redford's equality claim) or *non-sequiturs* (Horner's let's-just-fix-the-public-system remedy), which presumed public monopolies could heal themselves. The critical and substantive query to answer was and still is: How can regular Albertans obtain needed treatment in a timely fashion? An imitation of a system where the working poor have access issues (the United States) was never suggested nor sought. But a few dozen European countries make use of private providers, including payment for the same through government-financed systems. Instead of pondering reforms from outside of North America, most Progressive Conservative contestants for leader in 2011 chirped away about ostensibly superior Canadian health care. They were not only in denial but, as with some of the 2006 leadership candidates, again followed NDP messaging.

Et tu, Jim? The spiked flat-tax

One final bit of evidence that the Progressive Conservative Party was mostly bereft of small-c conservative instincts was how the party, in its dying days, set up Alberta's single-tax rate as road kill for the eventual NDP government. It did so by again mimicking progressive criticism of a conservative idea: an opportunity-based tax system that still collected plenty of cash for politicians to spend but emphasized economic growth over redistribution in its design. Enter the last Progressive Conservative premier, Jim Prentice, who, as he assumed the leadership of his party in mid-September 2015, soon threw away the crown jewel of the Klein legacy. Prentice, as with recent PC premiers, also snatched NDP talking points, this time, on the flat tax.[a]

Late-era Tories had long signalled that the Klein promise that taxes would go only one direction in Alberta—down—was over. In his 2012 budget speech, Redford's finance minister, Ron Liepert, hinted that "We need to look at our fiscal framework: at where and how we collect revenues,"—code for higher or new taxes.[25] By 2014, when Prentice took over as leader, the province's finances had been bleeding red ink for six years and, after a parallel decline in the province's assets, would pause for a year before plummeting again. Because Prentice's predecessors neglected reform on the spending side of the budget for a decade,[26] the newest premier looked for another way to balance the books: higher and newer taxes and a certain end to the flat tax.

Thus, after a succession of premiers turned a blind eye to the Leviathan-like increases in government spending, it was time to talk taxes—higher ones. With oil prices dropping, the premier said his government was "focused on making decisions based on sound, conservative fiscal principles."[27] The conservative reference was

---

[a] There is a technical distinction between a flat tax and a single-rate tax system. Between 2001 and until 2015, Alberta had the latter. A true flat-tax system would contain no basic personal exemption and tax filers would be taxed on their first dollar earned, an undesirable policy. No jurisdiction of which I am aware has that type of system. Alberta's flat-tax system was like many others described as flat-tax, a single-rate system (i.e., one tax rate of 10 per cent above the basic personal exemption). However, because is it popularly described as a "flat tax," I use that and the single-rate description interchangeably, also in part to avoid repetition.

easy enough, but given previous premiers treated fiscal prudence as the embarrassing, doddering uncle, the Prentice government resorted to what politicians often do in such straits: hike taxes and claim *that* is the difficult choice. It skipped the more serious work of reforming spending, which would put the government on a collision course with special interests in the public and private sectors. Instead, new and higher taxes were the preferred budget option for patching up the balance sheet, a direction that became clear in November 2014, when Finance Minister Robin Campbell remarked that "Oil is an important revenue source for the province, but it's not the only revenue source" and hinted at government action.[28] The premier followed up with specifics: the flat tax was to blame. Early in 2015, Prentice told a CBC interviewer that Alberta's current flat-tax system hurts the working poor. Prentice told the CBC that it "bites them pretty hard compared to the rest of the country."[29]

Prentice had it reversed. Other provinces taxed the poor far more than Alberta, in part because Alberta's generous basic personal exemption from income tax shielded them, whereas in other provinces, provincial income tax "bit" much earlier. His own finance department had written as much in the 2014 budget, six months before Prentice came to power.[30] In a budget section titled "Alberta's Progressive Tax System," the department measured the total provincial tax burden paid by the bottom 25 per cent of income earners across the provinces. The department analysis showed that the bottom quarter of tax filers paid 4.8 per cent of all taxes collected in Saskatchewan, 5.8 per cent of the tax burden in Ontario, and 5.9 per cent in British Columbia. In Alberta, the taxes paid by the bottom 25 per cent accounted for just 2.9 per cent of all provincial tax revenues. The finance department summed it up this way: "When all taxes are considered, Alberta has a very progressive tax system that compares well with other provinces."

Indeed, but other critics in addition to Prentice already argued the single-rate system was not progressive.[b] They were all wrong. The existence of a basic personal exemption means the proportion Albertans paid in provincial income tax was never the same but escalated depending on income. All this was obvious and trumpeted by previous governments. That included Ralph Klein's government when Finance Minister Stockwell Day announced the flat tax in 1999, and again when the newer Finance Minister Steve West promoted the single-rate system early in its first year, in 2001. Both ministers were clear on how *everyone* would pay less income tax, in part because the exemption was set high and the rate low. "No other jurisdiction in the country can boast such high exemption levels—the level a working individual can earn without paying provincial personal income tax," said Finance Minister West in early January 2001 when Alberta's flat-tax system took effect.[31] The Klein government deliberately added that generous exemption to ensure everyone paid less under the flat-tax reform: rich, middle-income, and poor, and it was why 200,000 low-income Albertans were removed from the tax rolls in 2001.[32] Yet here was Prentice, thirteen years later, claiming the opposite—that poorer Albertans were disadvantaged by the Klein-era reforms. That was false, as his own government's finance analysis showed. It was just that the critics, including the new premier, wanted even steeper progressivity—and higher taxes.[c]

The facts of the 2001 reform were not defended nor

---

[b] Another criticism was that the generous basic exemption could exist without the single-tax rate of ten per cent. It was true, but of a "so what?" variety. The point was that, with a basic personal exemption, the single-rate system was still progressive.

[c] The numbers surrounding the flat tax and its progressive nature are detailed in chapter 8. The current Alberta government and Premier Rachel Notley have made much the same claim as Prentice. The claims are incorrect.

communicated to the public by the last Progressive Conservative premier, nor did it matter in the budget to come. For months, Prentice dropped hints that his 2015 budget was a once-in-a-generation chance to "fix" Alberta's finances. The fix was in, for tax increases. In its March 2015 budget, the Progressive Conservative government imposed multiple, multi-year tax increases. They included higher personal income rates ($420 million), more in fuel tax ($535 million), and higher taxes on everything from insurance premiums and alcohol to increases in fees and fines worth another $700 million. In total, the new budget hit Albertans with $2.2 billion in new or higher taxes annually; an extra $11.4 billion in taxes and fees over five years; and no reform to public sector salaries, benefits, and pensions. (The government at least admitted *those* were a chronic budget problem which were driving up expenditures and restricting fiscal options.)[33] The newer and higher taxes from the Prentice government included a new tax bracket on incomes above $100,000, with higher rates and more brackets in future years, along with a high-income surtax and a health-care "levy"—a tax, based on income worth half-a-billion dollars. The various taxes meant that, as of 2015, the flat tax was dead. It was just a question of who would legislatively bury it. Less than two weeks after a budget with the most significant tax increases in Alberta since the 1980s, Premier Jim Prentice dropped the writ and called an election. The budget, presumably, would be passed after the May election, when the premier and his colleagues assumed that voters would return the Progressive Conservatives to power.

The Klein era: Hollowed out by his own party

Beginning with Ed Stelmach, the PCs disavowed many of the prudent and opportunity-creating Ralph Klein–era policies. It was the Progressive Conservative government, post-2006, that took Alberta in a policy lurch to the interventionist, ideological expensive left, be it on resource royalties, health care, spending and taxes. By 2015, the NDP could rightly claim they were only following the previous government, one with conservative in its name. From "fair share" language and health care policy that disdained private delivery even in a universal system, to attacks on the flat tax, Alberta's Progressive Conservative politicians signalled to the public they were little different from Canada's perennial interventionist political collective, the New Democratic Party.

Unsurprisingly, it was exactly that party who ruled Alberta next.

THE RECESSION IS OVER AND WE HAVE THE NDP TO THANK. PASS IT ON.
THE RECESSION IS OVER...
SOUP KITCHE
MAYES edmonton journal
artizans.com

2

Similar economic storms in 1993 and 2015

"Nobody would suggest things are great in the energy sector anywhere in North America."

Alberta Energy Minister Rick Orman, in 1992[1]

"I would hope it has bottomed out but I'm not sure."

Alberta Energy Minister Margaret McCuaig-Boyd, in 2015[2]

Claims, counter-claims, and facts

In late June 2018, as the summer solstice was about to produce its longest, sunniest day, Premier Rachel Notley tweeted her congratulations to her finance minister, Joe Ceci: "You're the best Finance Minister Alberta has ever had!" wrote the premier. The tweet produced the usual reflex responses from the supporters and critics.[3] But a few witty memes popped in, light-heartedly challenging the premier's Ceci praise. One cartoon character laughed so hard he coughed up his popcorn; a football coach unhappy with his team's performance yelled "Stop doing heroin!"; another meme showed Judge Judy with eyes widening and then her head sinking into her hands; yet another tweet surmised that the premier "must be into the hooch." Perhaps the best response from a Twitter contributor: "It's Father's Day. Not April Fool's."

The Notley-Ceci tweet was an example of the Alberta NDP's self-enclosed feedback loop, a circular mutual-admiration society where the NDP's management of the province's finances and economy were defended as superior to the Klein-era approach. Alternatively, when that seemed a stretch, when economic and employment numbers turned negative, there was a more defensive tack: to claim the Saudi-inspired, smashed-up oil market and financial wreckage left behind by the Progressive Conservatives made it much tougher on Notley and her colleagues to help the economy, create jobs, or balance the budget.

To wit, in early 2018, an example of the latter claim—that things were worse in the NDP's first term than in Klein's—came from Graham Sucha, the NDP MLA for Calgary-Shaw. Sucha, the chair of a legislature committee on Alberta's economic future, defended his government's record by alluding to the "context prior to both leaders taking on the role of premier." He meant that Alberta's main economic source of wealth, oil and gas, had been crashing just before and during the early NDP years in power. *Ergo*, Alberta's economy was in deeper dire-straits when the NDP took over, compared to the troubles faced by Klein and his caucus in 1993. To test this claim—that the NDP had a tougher time of it in 2015 than the Klein government did in 1993—consider six items in turn: oil prices, natural gas prices, revenue drops, interest rates, the budget hangover from high spending started by previous governments, and resulting "red ink" budgets.

Recessions, anti-Alberta politics, and low energy-prices

When Ralph Klein assumed the premier's chair in the wintry

days of December 1992, the province had endured three recessions in twelve years, a brutal two-year stretch between 1981 and 1983, a plunge in 1986 and another recession in 1991.[4] In late 1992, the province was also only then recovering from the lingering effects of policies that dated back to the 1970s and early 1980s. Those included the action by the federal Liberal government under Pierre Trudeau to impose a price cap on the domestic price of oil (after the 1973 Middle East oil embargo, which drove worldwide prices higher); a follow-up with the National Energy Program, in 1980, which restricted oil exports to the United States and so discouraged foreign investment in the oil patch; and the 1986 oil price decline after OPEC failed to agree on pricing, and which sent oil the prices of a barrel of West Texas Intermediate to $11.59 per barrel by July 1986—half of what it was six months previous. Seven years later, by the time Klein was in office, energy prices had risen, slightly, but were not yet high by anyone's calculation.

When Rachel Notley became premier in May 2015, there had been one recession in twelve years (2008-2009) and another had just started in 2015. The premier's early years, similar to those of her immediate predecessors, were also not helped by politics. The Keystone XL pipeline had been blocked by American President Barack Obama with multiple delaying tactics that turned into an outright refusal in his last two years. Foreign-funded activism and (some) domestic opposition to the oil sands also meant it was increasingly difficult to send Alberta oil to other markets, at least through pipelines. With the arrival of Justin Trudeau's Liberal government in late 2015, the Northern Gateway pipeline project was soon cancelled because of his government's ban on oil-tanker traffic on British Columbia's north coast. It was a project to which the Alberta NDP had anyway been opposed. In mid-2017, Trans

Canada's Energy East was cancelled after opposition in Quebec, and after $1 billion had already been spent to satisfy regulators but with costly new outlays expected from proposed new federal regulations. When British Columbia's New Democrats won power in 2017 with the Green Party in a supporting legislature role,[5] the Trans Mountain pipeline now faced a government opponent in Victoria in addition to protests, hurdles, and blockades. After the pipeline's corporate owner, Kinder Morgan, threatened to scuttle the project entirely in the spring of 2018, and with the federal government needing to show it could get at least one pipeline built, Ottawa bought the project for $4.5 billion. Taxpayers now owned a project that in late August 2018 ran into another roadblock: a federal court decision that ruled the federal government relied on an allegedly incomplete National Energy Board review of the project. At that point, Premier Notley, who introduced a comprehensive carbon tax in 2017 in exchange for hoped-for social licence, said she was angry and that "Albertans were angry," and cancelled further increases in the carbon tax. She also pulled out of the federal climate change plan, calling the decision and its consequences for Alberta's economy a "crisis."[6]

Revenue drops vs. interest rates

It is axiomatic that the price of oil and gas matters to Alberta government and its budget, just as American and Asian economies matter to Hawaii's tourist trade and the state treasury. In Alberta, the steepest year-over-year drop in resource revenues took place in just one year, between 2015 and 2016, when energy revenues plunged by 69 per cent. That beat the previous carnival ride–like drop of 61 per cent between 1986 and 1987. In this instance, the

Notley government had the tougher challenge, hit by collapsing revenues that made it more difficult to balance the books. For Klein, the first year in which he was premier actually saw a slight uptick in resource revenues, followed by two more helpful years in 1994 and 1995 before the money from oil and gas again dropped by 18 per cent. Between 1993 and 1995 inclusive, the years in which a reduction in government spending would occur under Ralph Klein, the price of oil averaged $26.62, with natural gas prices averaging $2.57. During Premier Notley's first three years, a barrel of oil averaged $35.71, with natural gas at $2.17.[8]

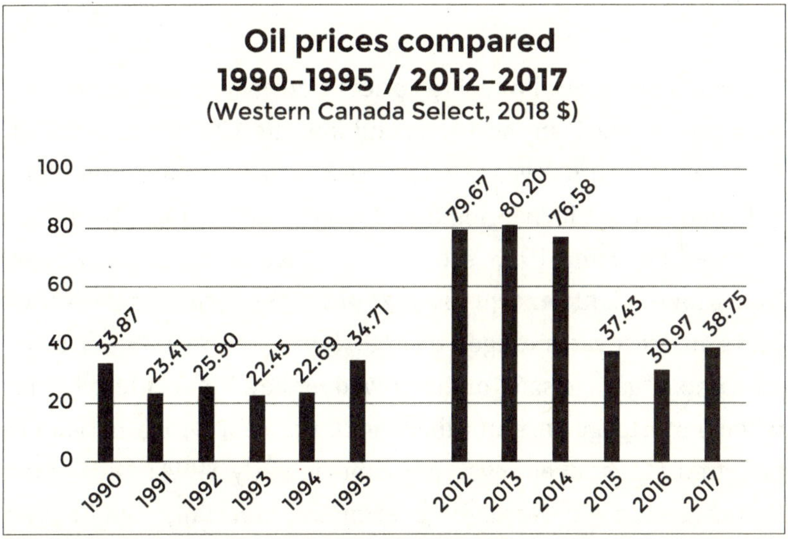

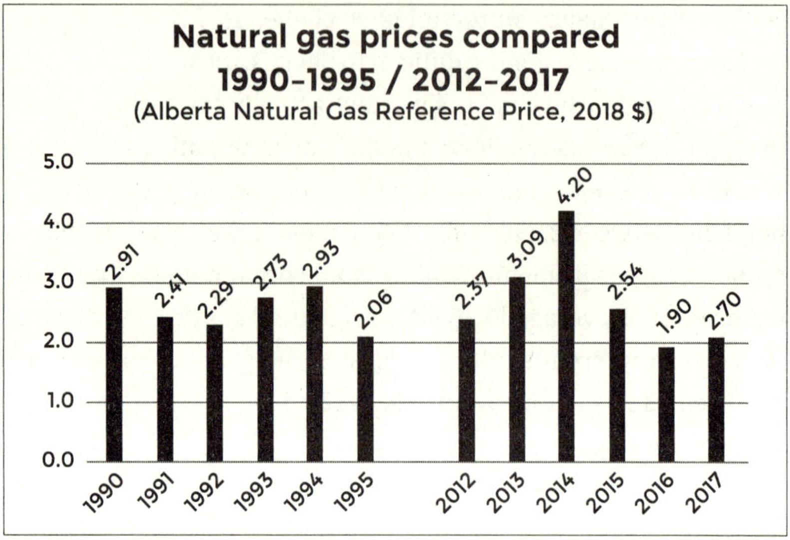

For Ralph Klein, low energy prices were matched by a perennial economic nemesis in the 1980s and into the 1990s: the high cost of money. Just three years before Klein came to power, the Bank of Canada was still charging double-digit interest rates (in 1990). Between 1990 and 1995, the central bank's interest rates ranged from a low of 3.88 per cent to a high of 14.05 per cent. In the Notley years, interest rates ranged from 0.75 per cent to 1.25 per cent,[9] a veritable "garage sale" on borrowed money. Klein entered office when a mortgage cost an Albertan 10 per cent with a bargain to be found at just over seven per cent (in early 1994). During the first three years of Notley's government, Albertans could obtain a mortgage for half that or less.[10] In the Klein years, significantly higher interest rates were the norm. During the Notley years, spend-happy governments, businesses, and consumers could all borrow on the cheap.

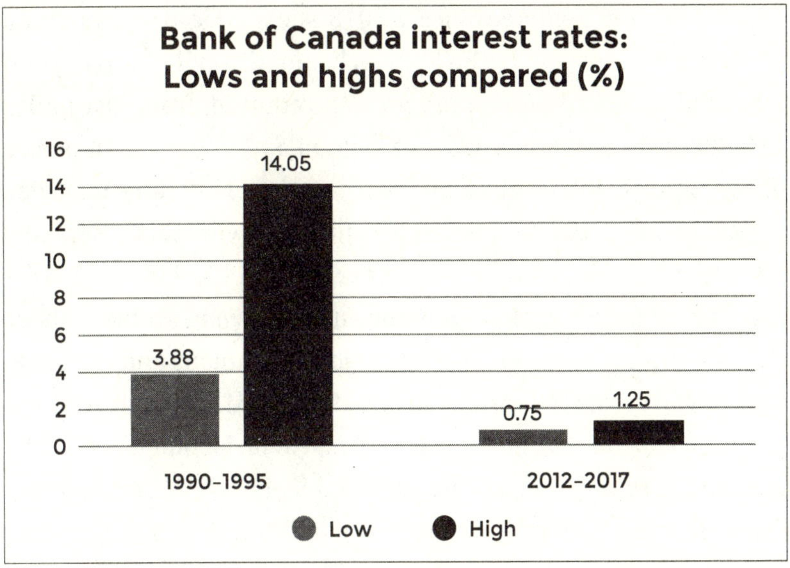

Sympathy for (the effect of) the spenders

Both premiers faced budgets that were made all the more challenging by the high-spending premiers that preceded them. In Klein's case, government expenditures had been reduced (somewhat) from the nosebleed levels of $13,169 per person in 1986 under Premier Don Getty, but were still historically high.[11] Per-person program spending dropped steadily for six years—something for which his government received little credit at the time due to failing loans to businesses and also chronic missed-targets on balanced budgets. However, the Getty government hiked spending in the year Klein came to power (the budget year that ended in March 1993). That, along with a growing debt financed with relatively high interest rates, was the challenge faced by Klein.

When Notley entered office in 2015, she was faced with program spending that rose under Ed Stelmach and Alison Redford beyond what inflation and population growth required, from just under $10,800 per person in 2007 to a high of $13,400 in 2014 before dropping again in the "hand-off" year when the NDP came to power, to just over $12,300 per person. The first NDP year was essentially flat—for program spending—but rose to just over $13,000 by 2018.[12] All of that understates the spending and borrowing problem under the late-era Progressive Conservative government and the NDP: both began to raid the various savings funds and also borrowed and spent heavily on the capital side of the provincial budget. It is why the funds began to empty out under Ed Stelmach, Alison Redford, Dave Hancock (the interim premier), and Jim Prentice, and then were drained completely under the NDP.

Both Klein and Notley were arguably part of the initial problem. Klein was in caucus and cabinet as part of the Don Getty government after 1989, the same regime which threw money at diversification projects that would later flop and cost the province $2.3 billion. The opposition Liberals under Laurence Decore, a former Edmonton mayor, consistently made the case that the Tory government was in an over-spending, fiscal mess of their own design—an accurate charge. Rachel Notley was a lifelong New Democrat whose party had been reflexively critical of any reductions to government spending in the 1990s and ever since; so the new premier, post-2015, could hardly complain about previous PC government indulgences on that side of the fiscal ledger. As a matter of principle, Notley thought governments should tax and spend more—and borrow much more. It is in part how she defines compassion.

The Ralph and Rachel welcome: (Almost) seven years of red ink[a]

For Klein, reduced resource revenues since the mid-1980s, still-high program spending and relatively high interest rates resulted in a fiscal train wreck, one still barrelling down the tracks towards the debt cliff when he became premier in December 1992. There were already seven consecutive deficits on the books. When Rachel Notley entered the office of premier, she faced nearly the same situation: six deficits with a tiny-surplus year of $22 million in 2015. True, the defeated Progressive Conservative government claimed a higher surplus, over $1.1 billion; but that claim resulted from that government's revised accounting that ended a more defensible definition of surpluses and deficits since 1993.[b] If the straightforward Klein-era approach was used[13], Alberta incurred six deficits and a barely break-even budget just before the NDP took power. For the NDP, that was a better scenario than the $5.9 billion deficit Klein faced in December 1992 when he became premier. Still, with steep drop in oil prices in 2015 akin to the 1986 swoon, the

---

[a] To give the reader apple-to-apple comparisons between the Klein and Notley era, most figures are converted to 2018 dollars and flagged in the charts. The exception is when a government is discussed in isolation as the inflation difference between 1993 and 1995, or 2015 and 2018, is minimal. Also, when examining the 1990s, for example, significantly larger numbers will seem out of place, sort of like describing the price of a bottle of Coca-Cola in 1950 as three dollars. Inflation adjustments between decades is necessary to grasp the relative magnitude of a deficit or debt; it seems superfluous to insert such numbers outside of such comparisons.

[b] The Klein-era approach was simple: if the province spent more than it received, that was a deficit; if it spent less than it received in taxes, fees, and other revenues, the province was in surplus. Premier Alison Redford's government hived off capital spending and amortized it. That meant overall debt could increase and, so long as operating expenses and operating spending matched up, the PC government could claim a surplus, which they did in the budget year that ended in March 2015.

Notley government had no economic May Day of a picnic either after its 2015 election victory. The NDP government also faced a severe budget crisis not of its own making, at least initially.

In 1993 and 2015, two Alberta premiers faced similar economic and fiscal challenges: low or declining energy prices, a weak economy and relatively high government spending by their predecessors. The differences: Notley was forced to grapple with a steeper oil-price drop just as she entered office and anti-Alberta policies from politicians elsewhere in the country; Klein played cleanup for every fiscal problem the Progressive Conservatives let lapse or exacerbated since 1986 and faced significantly higher interest rates with a greater proportion of tax dollars funnelled to debt interest. Both Ralph Klein and Rachel Notley showed up for "game day." The key difference was in how each politician responded once up to bat.

Business investment in Alberta

Business investment is what creates employment, incomes, and ultimately tax revenues for governments. Alberta prospers when a substantial inflow of such capital occurs. The following graph shows inflation-adjusted business investment (non-residential) over nearly four decades.

In the 1980s, investment in the province slumped due to various factors, including unhelpful federal policy and also weak oil prices in selected years. The investment flows began to rise in the Klein years; for example, by 1998, business investment in the province was $24.4 billion, more than double the 1992 figure of $11.6 billion. It was why Alberta was again described as "booming," even though significantly more investment dollars were to arrive in future years. It is critical for governments—be they in Edmonton or Ottawa—to ensure that Alberta attracts such investment flows.

MAYES
Edmonton
Journal
artizans.com
YOU MISSED A SPOT...
CARBON LEVY
PST
CECI

3

A core NDP belief: Albertans are undertaxed

"Making Alberta's overall tax system comparable with other provinces could bring in an extra $10 billion to $18 billion per year."

Gil McGowan, Alberta Federation of Labour, in 2010[1]

Charge of the carbon tax brigade

In the chronicling of famous battles, military historians will point to a number of examples of campaign failures, where, with some foresight, commanders might not have lost entire armies. One example: Napoleon's invasion of Russia, which required the 650,000-strong French army to not only find and defeat Tsar Alexander I's army—a chronic problem as they kept escaping—but to win Moscow and survive the Russian winter, which they did not. Another comes from Agincourt, where Henry V's much smaller English force defeated the French army under Charles d'Albret in 1415. Problems for the French included too-heavy armour on a crowded muddy battlefield, a disorganized commander, and French forces who mistakenly thought they were superior to the English. After the English initiated the battle, superior longbow arrows, better organization, professional and well-financed soldiers, and a charismatic king who led the charge, resulted in a French defeat. The men were cut down and into pieces by the advancing English.

If a common link exists in both military failures, it is the obsession by those in command to stick to some existing notion at all costs. Napoleon wanted Tsar Alexander I to sign a peace treaty that would have eliminated English trade with Russia; Charles d'Albret allowed himself to be drawn into battle when he should have backed away and allowed the English to advance to the coast and Calais. Which is where we might consider another not-so-magnificent obsession, and a hill New Democrats apparently wish to defend: their decades-long belief that Albertans are dramatically undertaxed.

The NDP's message to Albertans: Tax yourselves more

The examples of this obsession are plentiful. In 1993, the NDP platform demanded new taxes on anyone earning over $80,000 plus higher business taxes. "We can no longer afford to be a tax haven for the rich," said Alberta NDP Leader Ray Martin, just as the election campaign started.[2] Except the NDP leader skipped a relevant, recent fact: Don Getty's government had already increased personal and business taxes substantially, in 1987. Also, in the 1992 budget, the provincial government doubled the corporate tax rate from 6 per cent to 12 per cent, an increase that Klein never reversed.[3] By 1993, spending cuts were the only option left for an Alberta government after years of tax increases and red ink budgets. The class warfare call to the battlefield fell flat, and in the election that year, the NDP vote dropped to 108,883 votes, half that of the 217,972 ballots cast for it in 1989. The party lost every one of its 16 seats held in the legislature before dissolution.[4]

In 1997, the newest NDP leader (after Ross Harvey who served from 1994 to1996), Pam Barrett, avoided another rush into the muddy field of tax hikes but did campaign on a platform titled "We're fighting back!"[5] New Democrats railed against the reductions in provincial spending—the ones the public endorsed in 1993. In 1997, the NDP again dropped in popularity at election-time, to 83,292 votes. Similarly, in 2001, just as the Progressive Conservative government cut taxes and moved to a single 10-per-cent rate, NDP Leader Raj Pannu thought he spotted a winning strategy on the political battlefield: Divide and tax by class. Pannu observed that 80 per cent of Albertans made under $60,000, "so why not tax the rest?"[6] The 2001 platform proposed one billion dollars in new and higher taxes and $2.3 billion in new spending. The platform awkwardly called for a "more fair" income tax system with five tax brackets. Votes cast for the NDP dropped to 81,339 in the 2001 election.

In 2004 the NDP platform under leader Brian Mason avoided targeting individuals for tax hikes though he demanded an end to planned business tax relief. (On the flip side, the NDP leader did call for the elimination of health-care premiums.[7]) In 2008 the party was back with calls for higher resource royalties.[8] "Albertans deserve better than bargain-basement royalty rates," proclaimed Mason in his newest election launch, musing that "If Alberta adopted Alaska royalty rates, it would generate over $4 billion in extra revenue." The NDP promised to spend half that every year, $20 billion over ten years to subsidize green energy.[9] The results for New Democrats in 2004 and 2008 were 90,829 and 80,578 votes, respectively. In 2012, personal tax hikes were again back on the NDP front-burner and in the party platform. Under Mason again, higher-tax hopes sprang eternal and the party tacked back to the fairness schtick:

"It's time for everyone to share fairly in our province's prosperity," stated the NDP platform. The NDP saw more government, higher taxes, and a just society as inextricably linked. It lectured readers that it was "time that businesses and individuals with the greatest wealth pay more to support the services we all need." In 2012 the NDP price tag to fix the problem of undertaxed Albertans: $3 billion in new taxes.[11] In the election, when Alberta's population was nearly 3.9 million, New Democrats managed to attract about 18,000 more ballots than they did in 1993, this in a province where the population soared by 1.2 million in the intervening 19 years.

Softening up the public

Over the years, NDP allies repeated the same message, that Albertans were dramatically undertaxed. In 2010, Gil McGowan, president of the Alberta Federation of Labour, wrote how "Making Alberta's overall tax system comparable with other provinces could bring in an extra $10 billion to $18 billion per year."[12] In 2013, the University of Alberta's Parkland Institute argued that Albertans could tax themselves by $11 billion more and "remain the country's lowest-tax jurisdiction."[13] The NDP itself followed the rationale in both 2012 under Mason and again in 2015 under its newest leader, Rachel Notley. They skipped the scary 11-figure estimates of what it would take to tax Alberta just like any other province; but Notley promised to right the supposed Klein-era tax wrongs. "The PCs failed to earn Albertans' full and fair value" on royalty rates, proclaimed the platform authored in Notley's name. The NDP promised to fix that, and for the wealthy and business to "contribute a little bit more."[14] Similar to Raj Pannu in 2001, no one could accuse Notley of hiding plans for higher taxes, the carbon tax the notable exception. Four new brackets for undertaxed Albertans were proposed, plus a hike in business taxes.

Class warfare in Alberta: A failure to launch

The various appeals to tax Albertans ever-higher repeatedly failed to inspire a rush to the polls, including, arguably, in 2015. Over two decades, the NDP's high-tax platforms and anti-Ralph Klein positioning was ignored by a plurality of the public and some in the media as the ravings of a hard-left party with no chance of taking power. After the NDP's 1993 election wipeout, interim NDP Leader Ross Harvey was offside with much of the public, who wanted cuts to government spending to balance the budget and not new and higher taxes. He was unreceptive to the message. In February 1994 at a party convention, Harvey reiterated the NDP position: Its "fair taxation" policy would stay. The implicit message was that if only Albertans could see the wisdom in higher taxes, at levels comparable to other provinces, a balanced budget would result.[15] In 1995, Harvey told a Lethbridge crowd that cuts to government programs could have been avoided had the province hiked business taxes and increased taxes on the wealthy. "There's a huge business tax advantage and it's hurting us," said the NDP leader, with reference to the reductions in provincial spending.[16] The NDP leader ignored the obvious explanation for his loss: that most Albertans rejected his party's view that the provincial government should remain unreformed and be given even more tax dollars.

In subsequent elections, between 1997 and 2008, the NDP vote never recovered to even the devastating 1993 wipeout levels. It took until 2012 to see any substantial uptick in the party's vote count (127,075). Even then, a limited government party, the Wildrose, blew past the NDP, garnering 442,325 votes that year.[17] By the time Alison Redford became premier, and even with her 2012 election win, it was obvious that an increasing number of Albertans were ready to vote a new party into government. However, given the results in 2012 and in 2015, where two polar-opposite parties gained ground, it is hard to make a compelling the case that the NDP's higher-tax platform in 2015 contributed to their victory. Anger at the Progressive Conservatives and a province overdue for a new party are the more plausible explanations. Nevertheless, in the election that would, finally, bring the NDP into power—83 years after the NDP's predecessor, the Co-operative Commonwealth Federation (CCF), was founded in Calgary, in 1932, and 71 years after the CCF roared into the Saskatchewan legislature under Tommy Douglas, in 1944—Notley's New Democrat's won 604,518 votes, nearly 41 per cent of the ballots cast, and 54 of 87 seats in the Legislature.

Happy Canada Day and happy higher taxes

After the May 2015 election win, the NDP was in a two-decade hurry to right Alberta's historic tax wrongs and it took all of 44 days between the party's win, and the legislation to actualize their long-held hope: That Albertans would finally face fair taxation. While the first official NDP budget was still months away, the government quickly corrected moderate-tax Alberta with its second bill in the legislature, *An Act to Restore Fairness to Public Revenues.*[18] In introducing the new and higher taxes, Finance Minister Joe Ceci used the fairness argument beloved by politicians who eagerly look at the wallets of others. "We are asking high-income earners and profitable corporations to contribute fairly to rebuilding our province," said Ceci, in announcing four new personal income tax brackets and a 20-per-cent hike in corporate taxes.[a] "This measure will create a fairer tax system and help bring fiscal stability to our province so we are not so prone to boom-bust cycles."[19]

It was unclear how higher taxes would smooth out the yo-yo economics of Alberta's resource-based economy; higher taxes in a recession were *more* and not less likely to dampen economic growth. Nevertheless, the October 2015 NDP budget hoped for $550 million from higher income taxes and $1 billion more from increased business taxes when fully implemented.[20] Ceci, as with the Progressive Conservative finance minister before him, believed the province could tax its way to economic equilibrium and balance the books. It was an interesting theory and a dubious proposition. Every *other* province already had higher taxes than did Alberta. What successive NDP leaders, their allies, and reporters and columnists who blithely repeated the billions-in-higher-taxes-will-balance-Alberta's-books claim never noticed, or cared to, was how every other province ran substantial deficits year after year *despite higher taxes on everything*. Since 1981 and to 2015, all ten provinces had, collectively, run deficits in 29 of 35 years with surpluses recorded in just six years. In contrast, Alberta recorded deficits in only 15 years but surpluses in 20 years.[21] Higher taxes never rescued other

---

[a] The tax increase is described here with reference to its cost increase, as opposed to the rate increase. In this case, the corporate tax rate was raised to 12 per cent from 10 per cent. To a business, that is a 20-per-cent increase because a firm that paid $100,000 the year previous would be subject to $120,000 in provincial tax, all else being equal. To describe it as a two-per-cent increase describes the rate but not the actual effect of the tax change on the business.

provinces from red ink. The NDP's fervent belief in higher taxes ignored the other side of the balance sheet, but they were not alone. Attention to the dry, boring-but-necessary details of government spending, from corporate welfare to public sector compensation, was critical though most often ignored by the chattering classes. Evidence skipped, the higher taxes became effective on July 1, Canada Day, 2015.

Six months to $2.4 billion in tax increases, including on bird watchers

The summer break allowed New Democrats plenty of time to breathe and consider other taxes that might be added to actualize the NDP's fairness doctrine in Wild Rose Country. It also allowed the new government to consider what to keep and discard from the March budget, where the doomed PC government itself offered up multiple new ways to tax Albertans. The NDP's first budget, in October 2015, scrapped one planned tax increase from the previous government (a new health-care tax) and a few fees. It countered those cancellations with the already-installed four new personal income tax brackets, higher taxes on insurance,[22] and more markups on beer, wine, and spirits. The NDP budget also upped the tax on cigarette cartons by five dollars and hiked the fuel tax on trains that passed through Alberta.[23] The province's portion of education property taxes was increased by seven per cent, though the NDP blamed that on the previous government.[24] Court filing fees were imposed for the first time on fourteen fees, from Statements of Defence to Family Law Act claims. The cost of speeding in Alberta was also increased; tickets would now clock in at between $79 and

$474. In addition, the government increased another 44 fees and fines, everything from tripled campsite fees (a $50 fee could now be as high as $150) to quadrupled land rent fees for some industrial users. The first NDP budget even raised the group campground rent for bird watchers at Lesser Slave Lake Provincial Park. That rent was quadrupled.[25] *Finally, Albertans would be taxed just like taxpayers in other provinces.*

The NDP tax hit made it clear that the fourteen-year "experiment" in Alberta's popular flat tax now was definitively over. As if to make the point in dramatic fashion, the tax increases were worth almost $2.4 billion annually when fully implemented.[26] But that was only the start. More would come to match the NDP's belief that Albertans were severely undertaxed. Helpfully, the newest tax to hit Albertans in a generation, since the introduction of the federal Goods and Services Tax in 1991, could be justified as part of a strategy to reduce carbon emissions.

The carbon tax cometh

New Democrat Leader Rachel Notley and her colleagues neglected to mention two words in their 5,095-word, 25-page 2015 platform: carbon tax. And there was a problem: by the time the NDP took power in 2015, Alberta already *had* a carbon tax, a move initiated by the Ed Stelmach government in 2007 to buy social licence from reflexive Alberta critics and anti-energy activists. While applied narrowly, that carbon levy was set at $15 per tonne of greenhouse gas emissions. After the 2015 election, the new government cobbled together an advisory panel on the matter in the summer of 2015, and it dutifully reported in by November.[27] A few months later, the provincial budget adopted many of the panel's recommendations and put a happy face on the next tax increase. Just as the rise in personal and business taxes plus higher fees were justified with multiple references to fairness, Alberta's wider, deeper, and higher carbon tax referenced the new government's leadership on the climate file. The new carbon tax, set at $20 per tonne in 2017 and then $30 as of 2018,[28] was forecast to bring in nearly $4 billion in the first three years.[29] And it would hit the gasoline pumps and natural gas for home heating on New Year's Day 2017. Automatic hikes were planned in 2018 and 2019[b] and presumably in future years if the NDP were re-elected.[30]

The slew of tax increases announced in the first two NDP budgets, on everything and everyone from carbon to corporations to campers, would cost taxpayers an extra $4.8 billion annually by 2019 or $1,111 every year for each Albertan. The tax increases would collectively amount to $12.5 billion between 2015 and 2019.[31] Presumably that might finally satiate the NDP's thirst for higher taxes and finally remedy the "problem" of undertaxed Albertans.

Except the experiment was not necessarily at an end. That hint came in a 2016 CBC interview in which the premier was asked why her government avoided levying a provincial sales tax. Premier Notley's response was that her party had not campaigned on the matter. Of course, the NDP never mentioned a carbon tax in 2015, one that would cost $2.5 billion annually as of 2019. That never stopped the government from adding it to the higher-tax mix once in power. On a provincial sales tax, as the CBC characterized it,

[b] In 2018, Premier Rachel Notley cancelled further increases in the carbon tax, at least temporarily, after a federal court judgment ruled that the National Energy Board had not yet consulted enough with First Nations nor accounted enough for environmental concerns.

Premier Notley "left the door open by asking rhetorically, 'In the long-term, is this a conversation we need to have? I think it is. But not right now.'"[32] Unlike Tsar Alexander I and Napoleon, the NDP leader avoided yet another pitched battle for her cause, but she still clung to her party's decades-long obsession: Albertans were still presumed to be undertaxed.

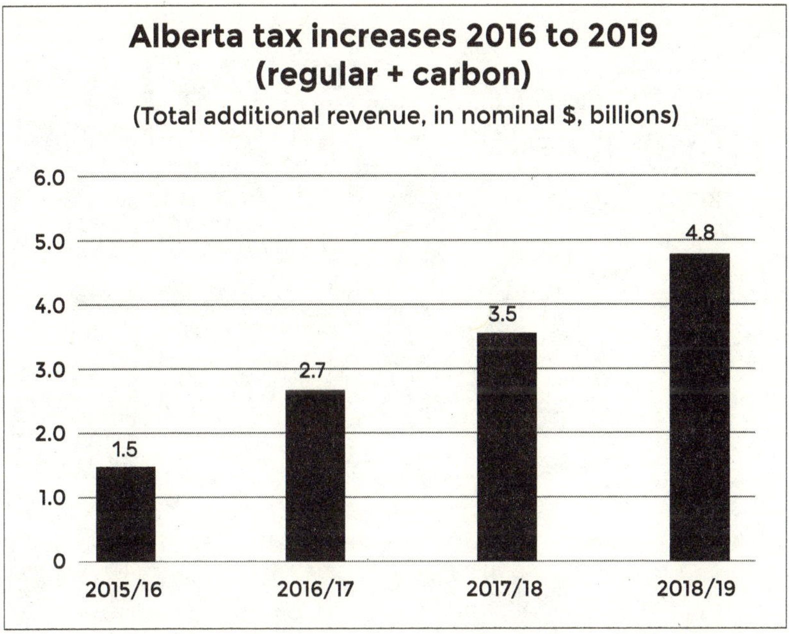

ARE YOU CERTIFIED TO WORK ON THIS?..
WHAT TOOLS ARE YOU USING?
MONKEY WRENCHES.
HACK KOFF
ALTA. INDUSTRY
NDP
artizans.com

4

The first temptation of Rachel Notley: Meddle

"It's not just a question of having a more fuel-efficient vehicle; it could sometimes be a question of taking a bus—walking, you know, those kinds of things."

Premier Rachel Notley, December 16, 2016[1]

Trickle-down carbon costs

End-of-the-year news conferences do not normally land politicians in trouble. Reporters and columnists simply want filler so they can finish work early and, in the fading December light, pick up their kids from school and get on with last-minute Christmas shopping. In turn, politicians need not overthink their responses to questioning journalists. A simple "life is good, we expect an improving economy next year" would suffice, even if bland copy. But in December 2016, Premier Rachel Notley was asked when she expected the new carbon tax to trickle down to Albertans and impact their fuel, heating, and food costs. "I think it would take a little while," mused the premier, before adding, "Perhaps it won't trickle down at all."[2]

The premier was in error. The Alberta Greenhouse Growers Association estimated that due to the coming carbon tax, heating bills for its members would increase between 30 and 50 per cent.[3] Non-profits were also soon to bear government-imposed, higher costs. The Calgary Food Bank forecast its heating and fuel costs would increase by $35,320 in the first year of the tax It was equivalent to an employee's salary or the cost of feeding 147 families in a month.[4] But those on-the-ground realities had yet to hit home. When a reporter pressed the premier on how a carbon tax could change behaviour if unnoticed, the premier backtracked. Notley admitted that the new tax *might* be a problem but then hypothesized about how Albertans could adjust their behaviour to reduce its effects—the "take a bus or walk more" remark at the introduction of this chapter. It was how Premier Notley managed, in an Alberta winter just starting, to land in political hot water.

NDP interventionism

The premier's advice—let them bike or bus it—was impractical for most Albertans for much of the year and in most scenarios. Given that an Alberta winter can last six months, biking and walking for long were not realistic options for parents who need to get their children to piano lessons on a winter evening in December, or to hockey practice at five o'clock on a Saturday morning. A senior who must visit a doctor on a frigid February day is not likely to venture out by foot as if they were 25 years old. The premier's response mattered not because more exercise or public transit is a bad idea but because it symbolized a deep government-knows-best streak. The December 2016 advice was only one example. Governments by definition intervene, but the error made by some progressives is an uncritical, default preference for intervention where unneeded. It is akin to thinking that because a small dose of medicine will clear up a specific ailment, a double dose will ward off all ills. To wit, ponder the plethora of examples that arose in the first three years of the Notley government and that illustrate the NDP temptation to intervene:

- a new redistribution scheme, care of the carbon tax, that fit the NDP's class-warfare presumptions;
- more taxpayer-funded subsidies to business, including alternative energy firms and the petrochemical sector;
- a hike in the minimum wage over five years at ten times the rate of inflation, just as the provincial economy tanked and took down business cash-flow with it;
- the signal sent via legislation that teachers and parents cannot be trusted to communicate with each other on children's sexual matters absent the government hovering in the background;
- changing the labour code in a manner that made it more difficult for workers to refuse a union if alleged trickery was in play;[5]
- interference in AIMCo., the company that manages the Alberta Heritage Savings Trust Fund, and the substitution of political direction for best-practice investing and a subsequent decision to end the requirement that AIMCo board members have financial expertise;[6]
- an early shut-down of coal-fired electricity plants despite how that cheap source of power was already declining in Alberta, from 66 per cent of Alberta's power supply in 1996

to 43 per cent in 2013, and was to drop to just 10 per cent of the grid by 2034.[7] Instead of allowing a mere six coal-fired electricity plants to cease operations starting in 2036,[8] the NDP government decreed a shut-down by 2030 and which entailed a $40-million "transition fund" for coal workers, $195 million to coal communities,[9] and nearly $1.4-billion in payments to utilities that owned coal-fired electricity plants in compensation for the forced early closures;[10]

- micromanaging health care for the benefit of health-care employees' unions, all while touting one's commitment to patients; and, lastly,
- engaging in beer protectionism—this in a country founded on the notion that all interprovincial trade should be, well, free.

Consider two examples in more detail: 1) the NDP's approach to the $20-billion health-care budget and 2) an issue at the opposite end of the public importance and cost spectrum: craft beer. The NDP government unnecessarily intervened in both.

Micromanaging the health-care file

The first principle of inadequate service is relying on one provider, an approach none of us tolerates when we buy food. We assume that multiple varieties of the same product, offered up by diverse providers and sold in grocery stores in a competitive market, benefits us in choice, selection, and price—in the outcomes. In contrast, after 2015, the province increasingly used a sole-source provider approach to health care. That was a problem, because despite how self-referencing progressive politicians often claim moral and management superiority on health care, the reality is that they often over-meddle and to inadequate ends.

This interventionist tick was demonstrated soon after the party took power in 2015, and on something as basic as linens and clothing provided to hospitals around the province. That year, Alberta Health Services (AHS) flagged how bed sheets, gowns, and surgical clothing provided by government-run facilities were failing to meet top sanitary standards. Problems at the government-run facilities included aging equipment and breakdowns. An *Edmonton Journal* exposé noted how "Medicine Hat has been one of the most troublesome facilities, with a 4½-month shutdown of its old ironing system, a sewer line collapse, daily power supply issues and a roof leak that destroyed the electronics of the cart wash system." The *Journal* also noted how such government-run facilities were a danger to workers, with "the linen services department posted a disabling injury rate of 12.06 as of January [2016], well above the AHS average rate of 3.01."[11]

The AHS was concerned about the replacement cost of the equipment, a price tag estimated at $200 million and potentially siphoning money from what the NDP always claimed to favour: frontline services and procedures.[12] Rather than spend more public dollars for inferior service, the health authority thus planned to shift AHS facilities to private providers, ones already servicing Edmonton and Calgary. A June 2015 AHS memorandum described the crisis and the remedy: "AHS has reached a critical point where the only viable option for sustaining linen services that are core to patient care is to work with our existing [private] linen contract provider and transition AHS facilities to them as effectively as possible."[13] The

AHS pointed out that governments in Saskatchewan, Quebec, Ontario, and British Columbia all outsourced linen and laundry services.

That preferred higher-quality, cost-saving solution was spiked a few months later by the new NDP Health Minister, Sarah Hoffman, who in late 2015 overruled the AHS plan. That decision to overrule the AHS only became public in August 2016 after the *Journal's* story. In denying the transition to more private laundry-services, Hoffman claimed she simply wanted proof they were superior: "If you want to change the status quo, you should be able to present a business case, and I asked for evidence," said Hoffman, after the story broke.[14] Except that the case *had* been made by the AHS—a year earlier; Hoffman simply ignored it. In a convoluted explanation that laid bare the real reason, the government's ideology, Hoffman explained the decision this way: "It lacks understanding of the current government that we want to make sure we consider a variety of options and that was one of the reasons I asked them to stop with the privatization agenda on this." In other words, despite existing success stories in Edmonton, Calgary, and in other provinces, the private delivery of laundry services offended the government-delivers-best ideological bias of the NDP as laid out in its 2015 platform.

Or ponder another example of micromanaged health care. In August 2015, Hoffman cancelled a 15-year, $3-billion contract awarded by AHS to an Australian company, Sonic Healthcare, chosen by the health authority the year previous to build a private facility and provide lab services in Edmonton. The ostensible reason for the cancellation was a complaint from Dynalife, a company with existing AHS contracts. An appeal board found that AHS's "duty of fairness" had been breached in the bid process. However, as AHS President and CEO Vickie Kaminski pointed out, the ruling also found that the tendering process was conducted with integrity, despite the problems. The contract had been fairly awarded.[15] One year later, reversing a long-practised policy where lab services were provided by the private sector in Alberta, Health Minister Sarah Hoffman spiked a request for proposal process already underway and which already cost $3.7 million. In addition, the province was forced to pay the Australian company $805,000.[16]

Interventionist ideology vs. effective health care

The justification for the minister's frequent interventions in AHS was always the same: that the public would suffer. "I'm of the opinion that this would have been an experiment," said Hoffman in 2015 when she cancelled the $3 billion private lab contract. "I'm not prepared to experiment with people's health and well-being." Except the minister did just that in her laundry decision that sheltered substandard, government-provided services. In that example, Hoffman was willing to spend more borrowed money rather than simply let the private sector deliver clean and deliver *laundry*.

The real reason for the chronic interference was noted by Kaminski, the now former AHS president and CEO, who resigned and forfeited a year's severance pay rather than continue in her role. A registered nurse with an MBA and forced by politics to deal with Hoffman, who possessed a master's degree in education, Kaminski left in November 2015, citing personal reasons. The truth came out the next spring with her leaked resignation letter: Kaminski quit because of micromanaging in Alberta Health Services by Hoffman and others. Kaminski's resignation letter explained how the "many (examples of political interference) are simply rooted in an ideology of the new government that does not allow AHS to do what needs to be and should be done." Kaminski offered examples of how the NDP government:

- interfered in contract negotiations with the Alberta Union of Provincial Employees, including reversing the previous government's zero offer to the union;
- vetoed the AHS decision to take over Calgary's ambulance dispatch services even though the health authority already paid $750,000 for a 20-year lease for a new call centre; and
- continued to interfere through Alberta Health Deputy Minister Carl Amrhein giving specific verbal directions to Kaminski for health-care system changes. Amrhein purposely avoided documentation to avoid—in his words—"any e-mail trail."[17]

Similarly, in ending private laundry services, even Dr. David Swann, the Calgary MLA and former Liberal leader who routinely decried private involvement in health care, thought the Hoffman decision was based in the NDP's anti-private-sector bias. "This ministerial intervention was based on ideology, rather than a solid business case,"[18] said Swann, who thought private-sector pickup, processing, and delivery of laundry was not exactly an existential threat to public health care. He was correct: it *was* about shielding government employees' unions from having to prove they could deliver a taxpayer-funded service better than the non-profit and private sectors. At issue was the protection of public-sector jobs represented by the Health Sciences Association of Alberta, with 144 members who maintained laundry services in Edmonton.[19]

Protectionist beer follies

If the NDP found it untroubling to interfere in a $20-billion health-care portfolio, this where every misallocated dollar meant longer lineups for patients, it was even easier to upend Alberta's beer market. That issue had great appeal for the NDP government, given beer as the "everyman" drink. It was also politically attractive for another reason: the government caucus had little private-sector experience and, if the Notley government could somehow "juice" the craft beer business, it would demonstrate sympathy for small business and how a mild dose of government intervention was just what the Alberta economy needed. That might help alleviate nagging public doubts about the government's general ideological proclivities and competence.

To grasp the needless intervention in Alberta's beer industry, it helps to know that when the Klein government privatized all government liquor stores starting in 1993, it also scrapped any cumbersome regulations on imports of alcoholic beverages into Alberta. An importer of beer, wine, or spirits could risk their own cash on what might sell. So long as they paid the provincial markup (the hidden tax on alcohol applied at the import stage at the warehouse), importers took the risk and reaped the possible reward. Also, other provinces' breweries, wineries, and distilleries were not discriminated against with higher markups just because they were located in Creston, Montreal, or Halifax. For 25 years, any Canadian brewer producing less than 20,000 hectolitres of beer annually could sell into the Alberta market at the same tax rate as locals: 20 cents per litre. It was a model of sensible policy, and it allowed entrepreneurs with a great beer to test it out in Alberta, serve consumers with plentiful choice, and potentially flourish nationwide and internationally if the new product was popular. Alberta was a free-trading nirvana and a test-market for beer entrepreneurs nationwide.

As of 2015, the free trade experiment in beer was over, perhaps another one of those "ridiculous 1990s ideas" that Premier Notley derided in a speech to partisans in early 2018.[20] In ending Alberta's come-one, come-all free trade approach to beer producers, the NDP government sought to remedy a non-existent problem. The government's approach to frothy suds was signalled in the first NDP budget, in 2015. There, the province noted its intent to refine the markup structure on beer "to promote made-in-Alberta products."[21] Refine was one word for it; gouging was another. All brewers outside of Alberta, British Columbia, and Saskatchewan were henceforth charged $1.25 per litre, a 525-per-cent increase over the previous markup. In the earlier March 2015 budget from the Progressive Conservatives, the province had already increased its hidden markup by 10 per cent and $75 million. The October 2015 NDP budget added another five per cent and $39 million, in part from the hidden beer markups.[22] That forced craft brewers outside Western Canada to dramatically raise their prices. After the October budget, one Montreal-based brewery, Dieu du Ciel, noted the extra taxes meant a three-dollar hike in the price of its six-packs sold in Alberta.

Other critics and an Ontario company later involved in the lawsuit against the province noted that the Canadian constitution prohibited any such favourable markup treatment based on provincial boundaries. The province soon revamped the beer tax to apply the 525-per-cent increase to *all* brewers "regardless of size or location." The province then publicly declared the problem fixed and that its tax-all-beer-more policy created a level playing field. Except the province anyway raked tens of millions of extra dollars from thirsty consumers, and, problematically for free trade, also used some of the extra-tax cash to subsidize small Alberta brewers. It was tax-and-subsidy protectionism, and it exacerbated a problem pointed out by Quebec's Dieu du Ciel at the start: how Canada's craft brewers could more easily export beer to the United States and Europe than to other provinces.

At the time of the revised policy, Finance Minister Joe Ceci claimed the new direction would diversify Alberta's economy and create more "beer jobs."[23] Premier Rachel Notley called the beer-tax move an "economic development strategy."[24] It was a standard defence used by politicians and governments the world over to favour a local business or sector, be it supplicants in aerospace, automobiles, energy, Hollywood film productions, or a drink made from barley, water, hops and yeast.

The political justifications always skipped the litany of failures, the lousy economics, and the perennial shifting of jobs and tax revenues that merely moved employment and taxes from one jurisdiction to another with no new net economic gains created. A subsidy to a craft beer maker might well create a few new jobs in Calgary but displaces brewery employment in the Kootenays, Saskatoon, and Montreal, exactly the intent of the premier and the finance minister. In such politically inspired job redistribution, Canada as a whole is no further ahead. It is a shell game and old-fashioned protectionism. The technical name for the practice is industrial policy, or "targeting" (as in targeting a specific sector for government support). The more colloquial references include crony capitalism and corporate welfare. None of it is new and the economic literature is overwhelmingly against the practice and has been since the 1930s.[25] But the Notley government, as with many grant-givers in government, rarely read (or cared) about such empirical diversions. They, as with many politicians, either sincerely believe that using taxpayer cash to favour one business over another is economically sensible or know it is a misallocation of tax dollars but keep it up as political theatre, for potential votes.[26]

The constitution and courts vs. the NDP government

Evidence on subsidy policy aside, the province was undeterred. The more pressing problem, legal and constitutional, was how the finance minister's protectionist fingerprints were all over the NDP's craft beer policy. As came out later in court, the minister wrote to the Alberta Liquor Control Board in 2016, asking the provincial agency to mark all beer up with the $1.25-per-litre increase "regardless of the production levels or location of the brewer."[27] He also wrote that the increase would "work in concert with an Alberta small-brewer focused program."[28] In other words: Apply the 525-per-cent markup to every company so the government can publicly assert it complied with free-trade provisions in the New West Partnership (the free-trade agreement between the three Western provinces) and the constitution. However, worry not! Alberta will send cheques to Alberta brewers to make up for the increase. And then there was the 2017 column from the finance minister in the *Calgary Sun*, defending the government's beer policy against critics. The minister wrote of his reasons and plan: "To foster economic diversification and assist an industry that was poised to grow, and grow quickly, our government implemented a grant to Alberta brewers."[29]

In the 2016 court case launched by two Ontario brewers, Steam

Whistle and Great Western, the presiding judge noted the 2016 letter but also an internal finance department briefing note given to Ceci that advised on how to sideline trade concerns and still subsidize Alberta brewers. The memorandum pointed to an advantage in this strategy compared with the original October 2015 budget beer strategy, how an Alberta-brewers-only subsidy would grant them even more of a competitive price advantage compared to brewers from B.C. and Saskatchewan.[30] The NDP government tried to game the Alberta beer market not only against central Canadian and Atlantic brewers; but they also happily undermined brewers in the two neighbouring provinces, Alberta's partners in the interprovincial free-trade agreement.

In court, the presiding justice, Honourable Madame Justice Gillian Marriott, found the subsidy program in violation of the constitution, specifically Section 121, which prohibits a province from enacting protectionist policies against businesses from other provinces. (The exact language: *"All Articles of the Growth, Produce, or Manufacture of any one of the Provinces shall, from and after the Union, be admitted free into each of the other Provinces.*) "The grant program," she wrote, "discriminated between craft brewers and craft beer based on provincial origin." She ordered the province to pay restitution of $164,964.98 to Steam Whistle and $1,938,660.06 to Great Western, the two out-of-province craft breweries who had initiated the lawsuit against the province.[31] The finance minister was in a free-trade corral, naked except for his protectionist "cowboy hat" and exposed as such by the court.

$2.1 million = 56,870 cases of Bud Light beer

That $2.1-million judicial rebuke to the provincial government paid for by taxpayers was equivalent to the cost of 56,870 cases of a 24-pack of Bud Light. The great irony of the fight over beer suds came from Premier Notley in July 2016. After Saskatchewan premier Brad Wall complained about the Alberta grant program for brewers at a premiers' meeting in Whitehorse, Notley, who lectured Albertans on the automobiles they should avoid in favour of a bus or a cold weather trot, protested Wall's pointed rebuke: "I will not be lectured about any efforts that our government might take... to support our small brewers, our economic diversification, our workers and our industries."[32] In true interventionist nature, and despite the Court of Queen's Bench's judicial rebuke to the Notley government's protectionist beer policy, the province appealed the decision in the hot, thirsty summer of 2018.

STANDARD & POOR'S
MAYES
edmonton journal
artizans.com
CREDIT DOWN-GRADE
NOTLEY

5

Reality matters: The Ralph Klein approach

"Albertans are no longer satisfied with the outdated and quite frankly dangerous theory that spending more money—even if it's borrowed money—or raising taxes and picking our pockets will solve our problems."

Premier Ralph Klein, June 1994[1]

Reality is an ally, not an opponent

Politicians do not normally think of themselves as architects or structural engineers, but it might help if they did; after all, architects are able to create buildings of beauty that can pierce the blue sky with a soaring combination of concrete, steel, and glass. Of course, before architects create a new addition to a metropolis, they must start with the basics. That includes working with structural engineers to investigate the soil beneath the proposed tower, this to see if it is sand, rock, or clay. That determines how a developer should then prepare the earth for the multi-story colossus to come, be it decorated with gargoyles, as if a centuries-old cathedral, or a modernist glass wisp.

An architect *could* try and design a tower minus the on-the-ground investigation of an engineer, except skipping that step omits critical data. It would likely doom whatever was built to a permanently faulty foundation. In short, reality matters: Is the proposed location near a river or an oceanfront that could flood? How strong is the wind? If by the sea, how much protection must be designed into the structure itself to endure Poseidon's hurricanes? Only after those questions are answered, and the physical constraints attended to, can the foundation be properly laid and a solid structure built for future generations to enjoy.

Politicians and others in governments can be akin to competent architects and engineers—but only if they properly grasp the core reality of a situation. When Architect William Van Alen and his engineers crunched all the numbers about the elements of the earth in mid-town Manhattan in the 1920s, it was not for the joy of algebra; they needed to know the reality of the ground below to ensure their proposed skyscraper could stand for centuries. For Val Alen and his colleagues, the result was the Chrysler Building—anchored properly, solidly built, and still around nine decades after the Art Deco masterpiece changed New York City's skyline. It is also why reality is positive, not negative. Build on that and the result is a thing of beauty that will last. Take shortcuts and disregard the numbers—ignore reality—and you end up with the Leaning Tower of Pisa. Eventually, the thing tilts.

Pisa and pre-1993 rhetoric in Alberta

Albertans were served up two very different ideological experiments in the last 30 years. And after all the political rhetoric, claims, and counter-claims are cleared away, what matters are the facts on the ground. If governments ignore numbers and statistics they dislike and become carried away by anti-reality ideologies, the public ends up with the bill for an unusable, faulty tower. Or, in political terms, politicians can spend of lot of time and taxpayer cash for poor outcomes and chronically missed targets—exactly what occurred in Alberta pre-Klein and again recently under Premier Rachel Notley. To understand what the Ralph Klein government faced in 1993, ponder the faulty fiscal foundations of the province, and public expectations for government action on the needed fix.

After the 1986 oil crash that pulled down resource revenues by 61 per cent in one year and led to a $4-billion deficit ($8.9 billion in today's dollars), government-by-credit-card became a regular pattern for seven years. At first, given the relative healthy state of Alberta's finances compared with other provinces, initial political rhetoric often emphasized that Alberta could "afford" deficits given other assets, e.g., the Alberta Heritage Savings Trust Fund. In 1985, in an economy recovering from the early 1980s recession but with a $671-million deficit, Treasurer Lou Hyndman noted Alberta's finances were fine; after all, there was the Alberta Heritage Savings and Trust Fund to put up against any new debt. "There are few governments in the world that can match the financial strength of the Province of Alberta," said Hyndman in his March 1985 budget speech.[2] "On an aggregate basis, this province is not in debt," he said, and that "less than one cent of every dollar we receive in revenue will be required to pay the interest on our debt."[3] Thus, the tone, given the memory of more prosperous times, was of unconcern. In June 1986, in a budget update after the oil crash deepened—and after the provincial election—a new treasurer, Dick Johnston, used language similar to that of Hyndman the year previous. Johnston told Albertans that "our per capita debt is by far the lowest of any Canadian government."[4]

One year later, the provincial treasurer did, briefly, change his tack: "We must take action now to realign the government's finances," said Dick Johnston in his March 1987 budget speech. "Deficits in the order of $3-billion cannot be allowed to continue. If not checked.... We would be passing to our children and grandchildren the responsibility of paying bills for the services we enjoy today."[5] But for the most part, the talking points from the finance minister and Premier Don Getty in the late 1980s were the same: We can afford to borrow from the future. In 1988, after repeated misses on budget estimates, Getty still downplayed the significance of the burgeoning debt. After yet another red ink budget, *Calgary Herald* Columnist Don Braid noted how the then-premier focused on Alberta's net financial position instead of the province's growing indebtedness: "Premier Getty was berating reporters Wednesday for recording these facts. 'Alberta is really "debt-free," [Getty] said, if you total up the province's assets and liabilities." Braid pointed out the obvious flaw in the premier's claim: "Technically, he's probably right. The province could likely raise $13 billion by selling off some hospitals, parks, and public buildings. The opulent Calgary Premier's Office would raise a few bucks, and the legislature would make a dandy loss leader. None of that will happen, of course. The thing that really matters is getting rid of annual deficits, and then the accumulated debt."[6] Braid was right and Getty was in denial. Alberta could borrow and borrow again; but it was akin to a pilot who asks passengers, while their jet was burning fuel at an unprecedented rate, not to worry, as the airplane was great at gliding.

Tax increases: Tried that already

Some attempts at program spending reductions were made after 1986; but the Getty government was chronically unwilling to face its flawed budget assumptions, or its deep-set belief that a government could rescue an economy with more spending.[a] The chronic budget misses on estimates shredded the Getty government's credibility. Meanwhile, that occurred in an environment with high unemployment and high inflation and where the same government was hit by financial scandals and bills from failing loans and guarantees in their diversification schemes. The government's basic competence—think of the architect who promises the Chrysler Building but delivers *Pisa*—was in question.

After 1993, some voices wanted the Klein government to tax the provincial budget back into balance. Then, as now, some economists wanted an Alberta sales tax, while others looked longingly at higher taxes in other provinces and saw that as the remedy.[7] Except that the higher-tax approach had already been tried, in 1987,[8] when the provincial treasurer was frank about the new strategy.[b] "We will increase taxes substantially at the outset of this deficit reduction plan," said Dick Johnston in his March budget speech.[9] The new imposts were multiple, massive, and included: An increase in the existing provincial personal income tax rate; a new eight-per-cent surtax on high incomes; a new "flat tax" on all incomes of one per cent; an increase in tobacco taxes and liquor markups; an increase in licence registration fees; a new hotel room tax of five per cent; a new fuel tax of five cents per litre on gasoline and diesel fuel; higher taxes for fuel used by airplanes and locomotives; a one-third

---

[a] This assumption is again popular but flawed. The province cannot replace the $30 billion drop in annual business investment. In 2018, Alberta's budget showed roughly $40 billion in own-source revenues so $30 billion in higher taxes to make up for the annual investment loss—to be spent by government—would crater the provincial economy.

[b] Before 1993, Alberta's finance ministers were officially known as "treasurers."

increase in the corporate tax rate; and more taxes on insurance premiums. The higher taxes were equivalent to 12.5 per cent of existing provincial revenues.[10] In addition, as of 1987, the province reduced and then entirely stopped resource revenue transfers to the Alberta Heritage Savings Trust Fund (the "Heritage Fund") and also re-directed investment income earned in the Heritage Fund to general revenues.

Still, despite the extra taxes and end to Heritage Fund deposits, the province incurred deficits in 1987 and beyond, this because Alberta's boom-era spending had not yet been substantively addressed. Moreover, the assumption that tax increases would bring in even the forecast revenue omitted their potentially dampening effect on an already-weak economy.[c] Ever-higher taxes added higher costs for consumers and businesses alike. It was hardly the strategy to encourage investment, the hiring of new employees, a raise in wages, or a boost in business and consumer spending. The public cannot spend what they do not have, especially in a relatively high-interest-rate environment where borrowing is also expensive. At least the provincial minister responsible for tax increases and red ink was occasionally honest about the over-spending problem. In 1988, Johnston remarked that "even with the expenditure and tax measures implemented in the last budget, Alberta continues to have the highest per capita spending on services..."[11] He stated the problem, but nothing substantial changed. The result was more budgets splashed with more red ink.

---

[c]Today, a tax increase of that magnitude—a 12.5-per-cent-hike in revenues—would equate to $5 billion, not far off the combined $4.8 billion in extra revenue the province expects annually in 2018 as a result of its 2015, 2016, and carbon-tax increases.

The end is near

Over the years, the Getty government had, on a per-person basis, gradually reduced spending but their main budget strategy was always the same: Wait out the bad economic news and multiple oil-price shock and hope it all reverses. The province was also famous for optimistic assumptions for energy prices and forecast budget revenues. In 1991, the Getty government introduced a budget that forecast a $33-million surplus in the next year, and added one billion dollars more in spending, just as another plunge in the price of oil hit Alberta. Provincial revenues dropped by 25 per cent in one year, not as deep as in 1986, but not nothing either. The avoidable action plus the unforeseen event made the already shaky balanced budget forecast wildly incorrect. In announcing the actual red ink in his next budget, in 1992, Johnston said the deficit was "of the same order" as in 1987.[12] The comparison was not far off. Five years previous, the deficit was $4 billion; Johnson's newest deficit was $3.4 billion. After another missed target, Liberal Leader Laurence Decore, whose party was first place in the polls, ripped into the treasurer. "Johnston's deficit predictions are so far removed from reality that one might think this is an April Fool's joke," said Decore, who demanded that the province quit "hiding behind falling revenue and admit that Alberta has a structural deficit."[13] It turned out to be the last budget for Don Getty; the writing was on the political wall and in early September 1992 the premier resigned. He was soon to be replaced in a nine-person leadership race, won three months later by his environment minister, Ralph Klein.

The 1980s are (finally) declared over

By Christmas 1992, just after Ralph Klein was sworn in as premier, most Albertans wanted what the government promised for years but failed to deliver: An end to deficits, spiralling interest payments, and growing debt, all of which imperilled public finances. It was same combination that acted as a fiscal wrecking ball, hitting government budgets elsewhere, in Saskatchewan under NDP Premier Roy Romanow, and federally under the Progressive Conservatives of Brian Mulroney, then Kim Campbell, and as of late 1993, Liberal Prime Minister Jean Chretien's government. However, except for the provincial Progressive Conservatives, the other governments never promised action for years, only to deliver ever-more debt.

By January 1993, Ralph Klein and the new finance minister, Jim Dinning, helped Alberta's Tories have a come-to-prudence moment. It was helped along by Dinning himself, who in the latter days of the 1980s-era denial prevalent among Getty cabinet ministers, was instead unusually frank. In 1988, Dinning, then the province's education minister, told a party gathering in Redwater that a balanced budget was at least four years away.[14] With the exception of the education minister, reality-seeking and the conversion to more fiscal prudence, were still rarities. However, as of early 1993, helped along by the new blue-ribbon panel appointed by Dinning himself, the Alberta Financial Review Commission, the Tories converted. The panel and its appointed chair, former CEO and president of TransAlta Utilities Marshall Williams, was given just 60 days to report back to the Finance Minister.[15] Two months later, the effect of multiple budgets from the mid-1980s onward that ignored the core problem was chronicled in the commission's report: "The province is spending more than it can afford, has done so every year for the last eight years, and the rate of overspending is increasing."[16] The Commission reinforced what most voters already knew and had demanded from politicians for years: Stop over-spending and balance the books.

Contrary to revisionist historical accounts years later that argued the Klein government hid its intentions from voters in 1993, the promise to reduce government spending was clear and set out by Dinning in May of that year. In the first Klein-era budget shortly before an election, spending reductions were the main tool employed to cut the deficit (with a rise in health-care premiums, one of the few taxes raised). The *Edmonton Journal* described the new approach: "Premier Ralph Klein's pre-election budget slashed spending by $703 million, raised health-care premiums and eliminated 700 more civil service positions." The capital city newspaper reported that Dinning announced "no tax increases, no new taxes and no giveaways."[17] While Dinning announced the broad strokes, Klein was more specific, calling on government employees "to be more productive and work with the government to find the best way to make cuts."[18]

Some expressed skepticism the budget could be balanced without widespread tax increases. In echoes of the Getty era, University of Alberta business professor Allan Warrack, a Progressive Conservative MLA between 1971 and 1979 and a cabinet minister under Peter Lougheed, was one: "I have difficulty believing that the government actually believes it is going to remove the deficit through expenditure reduction."[19] Some were apoplectic that budget reductions were chosen at all. A sociologist from the University of Alberta attacked the general lack of tax increases combined with spending cuts as "reprehensible."[20] Opposition to spending reductions came not only from academics but from some in the media. In a 1994 editorial in the *Calgary Herald*, the newspaper questioned the wisdom of spending reductions. The *Herald* argued "Klein was adamant that 'no society has ever taxed its way back to prosperity,' but he showed no evidence of any society which has created prosperity solely by spending reductions."[21]

The critics were in error. Successive budgets in the 1980s explicitly included spending as an economic recovery strategy,[22] but the economy was always weaker than hoped for by the spend-more advocates.[23] The result of attempts to stimulate the economy through government simply led to higher deficits, not higher growth rates. That was, after all, the lesson the 1980s taught in triplicate to Albertans: When a federal government intervened with the National Energy Program (NEP); when the Lougheed-Getty governments' chronic attempts to diversify the economy by public spending and government fiat led to 1990s' bills measured in billions of lost dollars; and from Ralph Klein's time as mayor of Calgary. The latter lesson was chronicled by political scientists Barry Cooper and Mebs Kanji who took issue with the claim that Klein was a big-spending mayor. They assert he was more prudent than generally thought at the time. It was, they note, under Klein that the city legislated a debt-reduction policy that would see debt interest costs drop from 24 per cent of the operating budget in 1985 to 15 per cent by 1994. Also, as Cooper and Kanji wrote,

> The chief lesson Ralph Klein learned as mayor, a lesson he was to act on when he became premier, was that a long-term solution to Calgary's and then Alberta's economic difficulties required *indirect* action. Klein saw that long-term prosperity

> could not be assured by government intervention; only the private sector could do that, Trudeau and the NEP had shown, however, that government intervention in the economy could certainly do a lot of harm. The role for government, he concluded, was to make it easier for others—investors, entrepreneurs, business people—to act. In that way the jobs of the secretary and the dump truck driver would be more secure.[24]

By 1993, Alberta's newest finance minister called on the deficit deniers to face the reality of previous, failed spend-more strategies. One media report paraphrased the finance minister's summary of previous assumptions: "Dinning... points to 1986 as the year it became apparent that Alberta had a spending problem. The bottom had fallen out of oil and gas revenues, the major source of government income. But spending continued." And the finance minister, in a late 1993 interview, traced it to the anti-reality disposition prevalent among some in government in the 1980s: "It was at a time when we believed a problem could be solved by spending more money on it. We've learned, painfully, that that thinking was never very accurate."[25]

1993: The politicians catch up to the public

A government that was unaffordable for Albertans and had already raised taxes and still ran deficits was the reality of what the Klein government faced in 1993. It is why that premier broke with the Lougheed-Getty-era consensus, one still shared by some in his caucus and party. Moreover, the public and the third-place Liberals (who topped the polls before Klein took over as leader) were demanding the same. One spring 1993 poll found that the provincial deficit was the top-ranked issue facing the government, followed by unemployment and then the economy.[26] A federal poll commissioned privately for the federal finance department that autumn would find that almost 90 per cent of the public wanted urgent action on reducing the federal deficit.[27] Alberta was not an outlier that year, and Laurence Decore's Liberals and Ralph Klein's Tories both knew it.[28] So the Klein government before and after the June 1993 election, which it only narrowly won, could look at the fiscal foundations ignored by previous governments and see that they were unstable, and anchored in assumptions that ignored local conditions, be it escalating debt or high interest rates. Klein's Tories could continue the façade that all was well, and prop up the province's fiscal Leaning Tower of Pisa, or rip out the structure, start over, and this time face the reality on the ground.

MEET MINI-ME... HE'S SLOWLY SHRINKING.
MAYES edmonton journal
artizans.com
ACCUMULATED DEBT
CECI
DEFICITS

6

Klein-era prudence and NDP pump-priming

"Alberta is now the model for other provincial governments and the federal government, which also face budget problems."

The New York Times, January 1, 1995[1]

"Alberta's credit rating takes another hit, despite economic recovery."

CBC News, November 27, 2017[2]

The 2015 Alberta NDP election platform with a smiling Rachel Notley on the cover was a masterful piece of seeming reasonableness. Barack Obama–like in its call to hope—variations of "Alberta can do better" repeated twice in bold print on the first page, the document was simple to read and in first person: "In this platform document, my colleagues and I set out our agenda for the next five years,"[3] wrote Notley to Albertans. She promised jobs, a diversified, 21st-century economy, honest and open government, and improved health care and education for all.

New Democrats even referenced—my words now—the shotgun shack-up between the opposition Wildrose Party's nine mutineers and their flight to the aging PC Party. In an almost-sunny manner, the NDP properly called the 44-year Progressive Conservative government to account for its arrogance, sloppiness, and almost divine-like belief in its right to rule. New Democrats promised Albertans a divorce from the late 2014 opposition-party/governing-party, December-May marriage that both party leaders, Danielle Smith and Jim Prentice, presumed upon constituents when they tied the knot. And while the NDP are often described as an accidental government—partly true if you believe the polling that posits half their 2015 vote was a protest against PC decrepitude and Wildrose ineptitude in late 2014—the fact remains that accidental is not illegitimate. The NDP offered a new political product; almost 41 per cent of voters bought it.

The 2015 NDP platform excised previous 1930s' throwback statements to nationalizing the commanding heights of the economy, including a government takeover of automobile insurance. But 1970s NDP tax policy was still there in all its psychedelic, 1970s redistributive glory. Being New Democrats, the Notley platform also promised new government-delivered treats for the public, and tax hikes on the richest to pay for it. "Rebalancing government revenues to make them more fair" by asking the wealthy and business to "contribute a little more" was how new and higher taxes were described by Notley's personal language.[4] (One major omission was the multi-billion-dollar, non-neutral carbon tax that would show up in 2016, *after* the NDP formed government.) The NDP purported to cost it all out, including how to arrive at a balanced budget. Thus, a patina of reasonableness looked apparent unless one dug down deep.[5] The NDP platform even promised to bring the budget back to black by 2018.

It was never going to happen.

A study in contrasts: Ralph, Rachel, and your money

Recall the Ralph Klein platform from May 1993: Spending reductions worth $3.5 billion over four years that amounted to a 20-per-cent reduction in the size of Leviathan, a balanced budget by year four, debt payback after that, and no tax increases in year one but no guarantee in subsequent years.[6] *Contra* Klein, the 2015 NDP platform pitch was based in a very 1970s–Pierre Trudeau and 1980s–Don Getty assumption: Higher taxes and more government spending could jolt Alberta into a recovery in the manner a defibrillator is applied to a stopped heart. Except a sluggish economy is not a nearly-dead patient but a workhorse that need less and not more weight on its back to gallop along at a faster clip. The NDP chose to add extra packs—taxes, to the back of the economic "animal." As for spending, the NDP platform promised $12 billion in new spending over five years in addition to what was planned in the March 2015 budget from the outgoing P.C. government.[7]

The diverse paths: Klein chose spending reductions across the public service, including a five-per-cent reduction in compensation, red-tape reductions, and privatization of government liquor stores and government registries. There was a default preference for competition over monopolies. The budget was balanced two years early, by 1995, an impossible feat absent the spending cuts and with only some luck from rising oil and natural gas prices. By 1996 the debt was shrinking, as were interest costs, and the Klein government enacted a limit on the provincial government's ability to be in business with business, a source of past over-spending and lost public dollars.

The Notley results: in power, the NDP government blew past its five-year $12-billion pledge and spent more than that in just three year ($13.5 billion). By 2018, the government forecast nearly $25 billion in extra program spending by 2020, more than double the NDP's 2015 platform promise.[8] The government also ended contracts with the private sector and replaced those with services delivered and staffed by government employees' unions. On another file, subsidies to businesses were always an odd policy for a party that railed against corporations and the rich, but the Notley government offered corporate welfare to companies in multiple sectors, from traditional energy companies and green corporations to brewers of beer.

Disagree or agree with Klein and his colleagues or Notley and hers, but to use a phrase from his 1997 campaign, Klein "kept his word." Candidate Klein promised a balanced budget in four years and Premier Klein delivered in two. Candidate Notley promised three deficit years and then a $25 million surplus by 2019.[9] Premier Notley's commitment was dead on arrival once the NDP gained power. In power, the NDP modified their balanced budget promise to 2020 and then 2023.[10] It was the late 1980s Progressive Conservative Getty government all over again, but in New Democrat colours. The NDP government blamed the balanced budget delay on the economy. Ralph Klein had similar problems in 1993 and a similar temptation. He delivered on his promise to balance the books.

Financial assets/debt

The NDP arrived in office with $14 billion left in the provincial "piggy bank," broke it open, spent the remaining cash, and turned the province's overall balance negative for the first time in 20 years. By early 2019, Alberta's net financial debt will be $30 billion, a $44-billion decline in just four years, with another $18 billion to be added by 2021. Previously, the deepest debt year for Alberta under Klein was 1994, when it reached just over $23 billion. By 1997, his government wrestled it down to just over $14 billion, a $9-billion turnaround to the good.[11] That had payoffs. By the year 2000, interest payments were $1.2 billion less when compared with 1995. As spending increased again after 1997, it was affordable and not placed on the provincial line of credit. To put it in business terms, new spending and later tax-relief were both financed out of free cash flow, not debt.

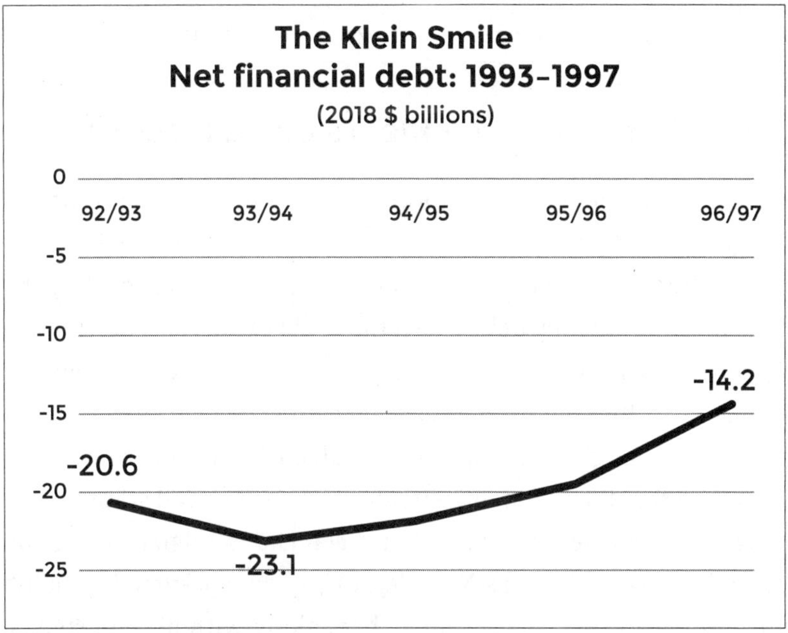

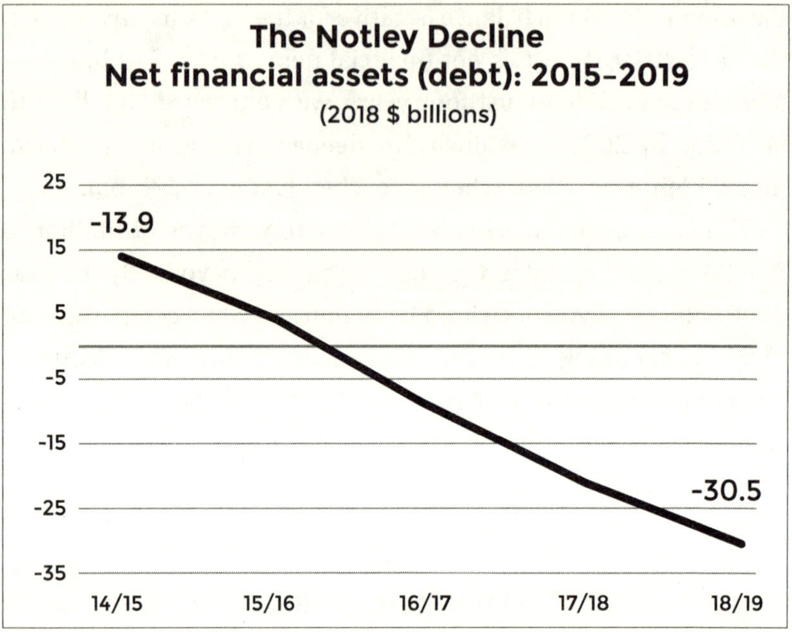

The $63-billion man: Klein's overall record

Expand the analysis to Ralph Klein's entire time in office, and the results move in the same direction: ever-higher financial assets. By the end of the 1990s, Klein could technically declare the province was already debt-free if the value of the Alberta Heritage Savings and Trust Fund was set astride the shrinking provincial debt. But by 2004, by any measurement, Alberta could be considered debt-free, a singular example among all Canadian governments. It was then that Klein announced Alberta's newly freed status at the Calgary Stampede. "Paid in Full!" proclaimed the sign held high by Klein. Two years later, as Klein left office, the one-time journalist turned mayor and then premier had, along with his colleagues, transformed Alberta's finances: deficits were a distant memory, the debt was gone, and spending was up—only this time not with borrowed money. The province moved from a debt "pit" of over $20 billion in 1994 to financial assets worth nearly $43 billion when Klein left office. The 1980s habits had been vanquished, early 1990s realities recognized, the agenda re-set and re-poured, and a new fiscal foundation built. The premier known more often as "Ralph" engineered a $63-billion-plus turnaround. The Klein government built a "Chrysler Building" on *terra firma*.[12]

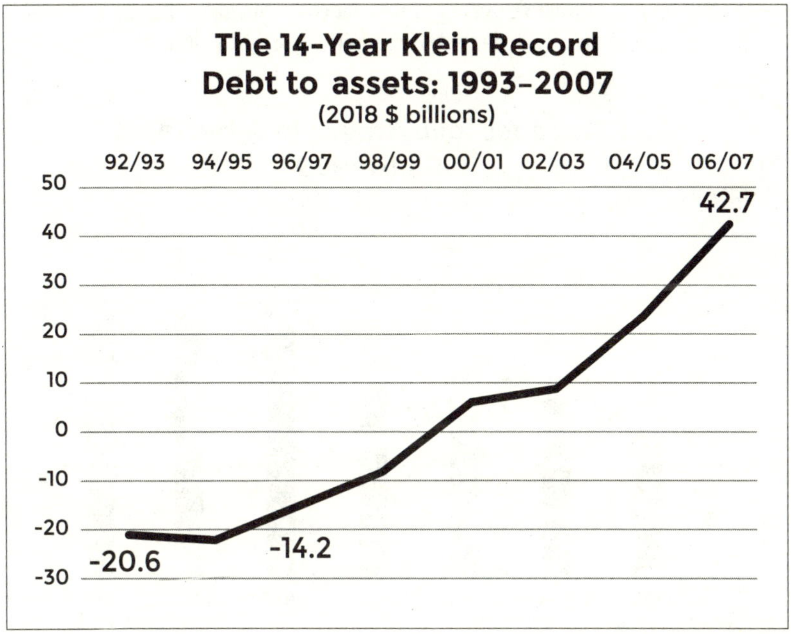

Zoom-zoom: Alberta's economic growth in the 1990s

In 1993, on the eve of the June election where the Progressive Conservatives were returned to power with a reduced majority, labour leaders told the media that Ralph Klein's reductions in government spending would result in a weaker economy and higher unemployment. In fact, in the 1990s, the province zoomed ahead and Alberta experienced the best economic growth in the country. Between 1993 (just as Klein-era policies began) and 1999, business investment soared and Alberta's economic growth was higher than the national average in seven of eight years. Overall, Alberta's average annual economic growth was 4.5 per cent, higher than any other province in those eight years.[13]

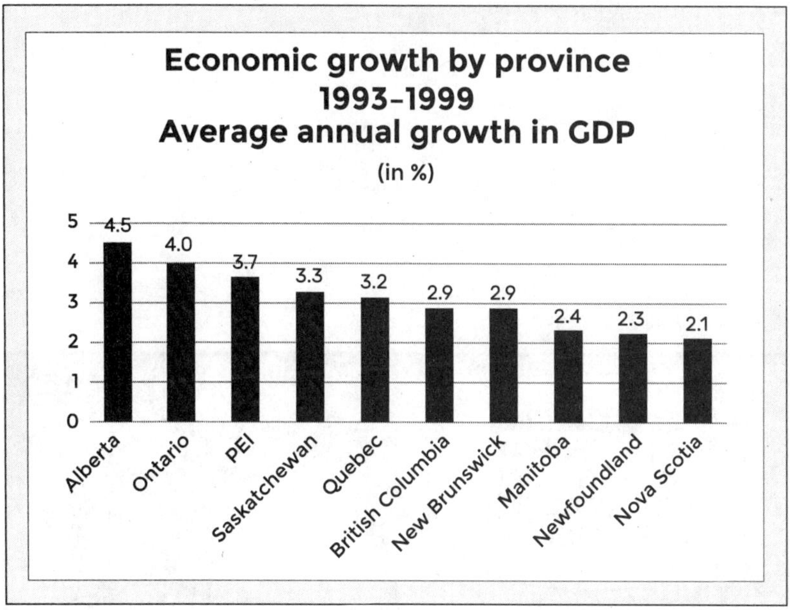
Economic growth by province
1993–1999
Average annual growth in GDP
(in %)
5
4
3
2
1
0
4.5
4.0
3.7
3.3
3.2
2.9
2.9
2.4
2.3
2.1
Alberta
Ontario
PEI
Saskatchewan
Quebec
British Columbia
New Brunswick
Manitoba
Newfoundland
Nova Scotia

WE'RE CHARTING A DIFFERENT COURSE THAN BRAD WALL AND SASKATCHEWAN.
DEBT
AB
MAYES Edmonton Journal
artizans.com

7

How Ralph Klein saved health care and education

"All the Conservatives can talk about is a bunch of government bookkeeping stuff."

Ross Harvey, New Democratic Party leader, in 1996[1]

"The debt and deficit are not inventions of ideology. They are facts of arithmetic. The quicksand of compound interest is real."

Federal Finance Minister Paul Martin in 1995, on why the Liberal government cut spending

Eroding health and education, one debt-dollar at a time

When in 1998 the Calgary Regional Health Authority blew up the Calgary General, the downtown hospital Ralph Klein was born in fifty-six years previous, journalist Don Martin would later write that the premier "didn't enjoy it one bit." It was not because Klein was sentimental about the facility; it was a nine-decades-old building, and its services would be transferred to other and newer city hospitals. But Klein "instinctively knew the spectacular demolition detonation... was an indelible image that would haunt his plans to tear down and rebuild health care in revolutionary style."[2] The premier's impulse was "absolutely right," wrote Martin, and indeed it was: 20 years later, the NDP government's Health Minister Sarah Hoffman was still tweeting footage of that October 1998 morning when 1,733 kilograms of dynamite razed the initial sandstone structure and all its additions into dust.

The 1990s Rorschach test

Health care and education, and the Klein government's temporary reduction in spending in both ministries was, and still is, like a Rorschach test for Albertans. Many people see what they see and cannot envision any other image. The reality, apart from whatever one recalls from then or reads about that decade now, is that when Klein became premier, government debt daily snatched money away from patients and students due to escalating interest costs. In 1993, Alberta spent over $1.4 billion in debt interest. In that year, it was equivalent to 33 per cent of health-care spending, 36 per cent of the budget for education, or 75 per cent of the money spent on social services. Debt interest was, shooting-star-like, headed up, to over $1.7 billion by 1995. And that figure came *after* provincial spending reductions in every department began and which prevented even more borrowing and higher interest payments. Another way to ponder that decade and this problem: Between 1985 and 1993 in Alberta, the cost of interest on Alberta's growing debt was $7.2 billion, equivalent to two full years of what the province spent on health care just a few years previous (in 1990).

That was the dilemma the Klein government faced in 1993, and mounting interest payments were forecast to rise unless budget expenditures were reduced, the deficit eliminated, the debt stalled, debt repayment begun, and interest payments set to "decline" and not "incline." Two decades later, the numbers are straightforward but the Rorschach rhetoric often still reflects, understandably, one's position then or now. As the late Tip O'Neill, Speaker of the U.S. House of Representatives once put it, "all politics is local." For someone laid off by a politician in the 1990s, or who faced a health care wait or worse, a numbers analysis two decades later is unlikely to persuade them to change their mind. Nor will it stop the use of the 1990s as a touchstone for present-day positions. In 2015, when Premier Jim Prentice proposed to curtail some expenditures in future years to help balance the books, United Nurses of Alberta President Heather Smith referenced the Klein era with disdain and extreme rhetoric. "We've done this before," Smith said. "We've paid very dearly for doing it." Smith claimed the Klein-era reductions "caused irreparable harm, perhaps even loss of life, to Albertans by taking a chainsaw to health and other programs in the province." On education, Mark Ramsankar, president of the Alberta Teachers' Association, also brought up the 1990s: "Teachers will not budge. We can't. The education system cannot take another hit like this."[3]

That rhetoric was unpopular among many Albertans in the 1990s because much of the public then, as now, well understood that the critics had the 1990s cause-and-effect backward: Ralph Klein's government was not the reason a child, spouse, grandparent, father, mother, or sibling lacked timely treatment in the 1990s or faced overcrowded classrooms. Nor could tax reductions be blamed as "taking away" money from the government's two biggest spending envelopes, health care and education. In 1993, debates about taxes and their proper type and levels were still in the future.

Instead, blame was better placed at the feet of governments that preceded Klein that focused not on what government can and should do but were chronically unfocused and thus borrowed heavily to pay for deficit-attention disorder. From so-called diversification schemes to the belief that a small economy on the relatively isolated northern half of the North American continent could spend its way to prosperity, anti-reality economics were in vogue in the later 1980s and early 1990s. It was only once government spending was cut that deficits stopped and interest costs were managed and why those payments relative to social programs peaked in 1995. The Klein government recognized the crisis. They also dealt with it. Few governments do.

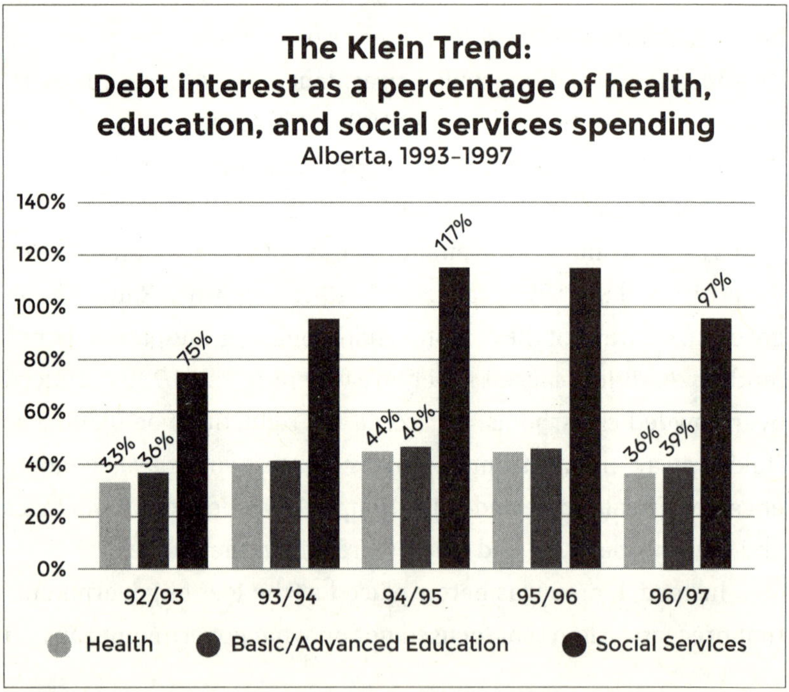

Cross-country concern

The debt crisis was not unique to Alberta. The public finance problem of interest chewing up tax dollars existed elsewhere and with governments of every partisan and ideological stripe. Debt interest payments were, as federal Finance Minister Paul Martin expressed in 1995, "not inventions of ideology" but "facts of arithmetic." Years later, in a 2018 address to an Ottawa think tank, Martin argued that the public accepted deep spending cuts if done across the board (to social programs and also to business subsidies) because they understood the resulting reduction in the deficit "was the only way we could protect our social foundation in the longer term."[4] In fact, Canadians were ahead of most politicians on the matter. They wanted spending cuts to deal with ballooning debt-interest payments. One autumn 1993 poll conducted for the federal government found that 92 per cent of respondents were "concerned" about the deficit, with 63 per cent "very concerned"; 87 per cent thought urgent action was necessary (to reduce the deficit) and 41 per cent saw the deficit situation as a crisis.[5]

Debt interest under Premier Notley

Over two decades later, the NDP still disdain the arithmetical advantages that accrue to balancing the books and define fiscal prudence as anti-people. In November 2016, in a speech to the Alberta Association of Municipal Districts and Counties, Premier Rachel Notley rejected any suggestion of a reduction to government spending. She told the crowd that "There are already enough families in Alberta worrying about how to meet the mortgage" and that "creating more unemployment and reducing more services won't make things better."[6] In 2017, at the Canadian Labour Congress convention in Toronto, the premier repeated the message: "From our very first days in government, we were confronted with a choice, would we respond like past governments and impose severe cuts to the services that families rely on?" The question was, of course, rhetorical and Notley answered her own query, framed to portray red ink as positive: "Our first commitment is, and always will be, to put regular people at the center of our decisions."

The premier then compared her philosophy with Brad Wall's Saskatchewan government, which recently cut expenditures to help balance the books, including plans to reduce public sector compensation by 3.5 per cent.[7] Notley criticized the Saskatchewan premier with the same language and images that her party offered up in the 1990s vis-à-vis Klein, and with an assumption that attention to "mere" fiscal issues was obsessive bean-counting.[8] In August 2018, in a mid-summer tweet, Notley again framed any restraint on spending as anti-people. "Budgets are about choices, tweeted the premier. "We made the choice to invest – in child care, roads, hospitals..." and then the premier's zinger of a non sequitur: "Some people say we should balance the budget as quickly as possible no matter how many people it hurts."[9] The binary, either-or choice ignored a third option, one unpopular to raise in polite public-sector company: Match private sector practice and require government employees and the broader public sector to make do with less.

Had she wanted to, the premier could find examples in Alberta, in the private sector. In 2014, after the oil crash began, in attempts to avoid layoffs, companies reduced wages and benefits to stay solvent and to keep more people working. In early 2015, Calgary-based

Trinidad Drilling cut staff salaries and management compensation by seven and ten per cent, respectively.[10] In the spring of 2016, after the energy patch had not yet recovered, Trican Well Services initiated a 50-per-cent reduction for two months. "It's basically to help preserve jobs," said Trican Chief Executive Officer Dale Dusterhoft in an interview with the *Financial Post*. "Instead of laying off people, we're trying to keep as many people as we can around with a reduced salary structure." But reducing public sector pay by just 3.5 cent as the Wall government did in 2017 and as the Tories under Klein did in 1993 (by 5 per cent) was never considered by the NDP government. Instead the premier defended existing government spending, which just happened to dovetail with the interests of core NDP supporters. It is why the province would, even in 2018, after four years of deterioration in private-sector employment and income, sign collective agreements with government employees' unions where future layoffs were prohibited.[12] This, the public was repeatedly told, was in their interest.

Reality check: Interest costs again bite into programs

Under Rachel Notley, Alberta raced back to the 1980s tactic of extending government spending long after the boom-time merry-go-round stopped in the private sector. By 2015 Alberta's finances had never really recovered from the 2008/09 financial meltdown; the 2014 and 2015 drop in oil prices only added to the fiscal disaster already unfolding and, while the Notley government was temporarily lucky with low interest rates, the long-term strategy of reliance on cheap money was debatable, but the consequences were clear: the province was loading up on cheap debt.

While economists, central bankers, and taxpayers in countries the world over wait to see if that ten-year experiment in low interest rates succeeds or fails, borrowing more and the compounding problem exists even with low interest rates. Alberta's interest costs and the effect on spending are not yet as dire as in the 1990s; but debt interest costs are again eroding choices. Interest payments were $722 million when New Democrats took power in 2015, hit $1.9 billion in 2018 and will be $3 billion by 2021. Soon even fewer social workers can be hired, it will be harder to reduce classroom sizes,

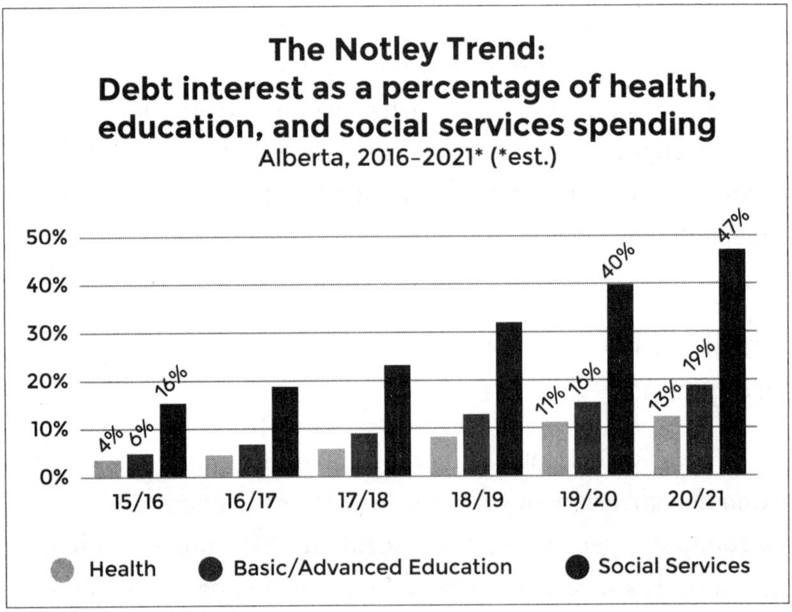

and the money for new doctors to tend to patients will evaporate.

The "No money down! Pay later!" fantasy

"My mother died waiting for health care treatment in the 1990s due to Klein's cuts," wrote one Twitter correspondent to me in early 2018. I have no idea if the tweet was honest, but some Albertans could indeed make such a claim. Others might recount problems in the streets or in education. But it was never Ralph Klein's spending reductions in the 1990s that harmed Albertans; that would blame the consequences of excessive borrowing and not the disease—the deficits, debt, and interest costs that resulted from any number of choices and events. Unlike the first three years under the NDP government where the interest bite again headed higher, under Ralph Klein, by 1995, the province no longer financed surgeries and salaries by borrowing from the next generation. Nor did the government buy textbooks and pay teacher salaries on a huckster-like, "no money down, buy now, pay later!" installment program. This was even more evident in the budget year that coincided with Klein's retirement in December 2006. By then, interest on Alberta's debt amounted to just $269 million, a fraction of the interest Albertans paid in the mid-1990s.[a] Relative to core programs, it was seven per cent of the social services budget, three per cent of the money flowing into basic and advanced education, and just two per cent of the health-care budget. It is time to re-take the 1990s Rorschach test: Ralph Klein's government saved health care and education.

---

a) The leftover debt and interest on the same existed only because of long-term due dates on provincial bonds. Money for the debt had already been put aside and thus the debt effectively wiped to zero.

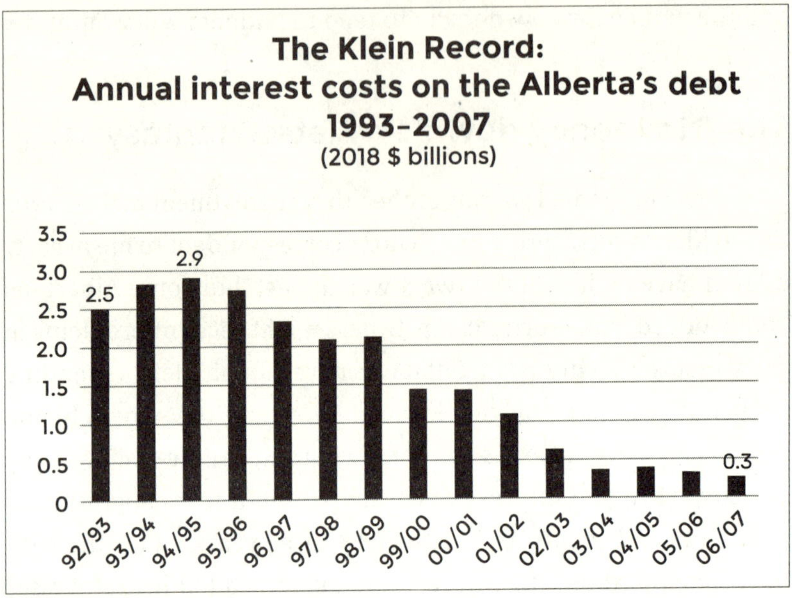
The Klein Record:
Annual interest costs on the Alberta's debt
1993–2007
(2018 $ billions)
3.5
3.0
2.5
2.0
1.5
1.0
0.5
0
2.5
2.9
0.3
92/93
93/94
94/95
95/96
96/97
97/98
98/99
99/00
00/01
01/02
02/03
03/04
04/05
05/06
06/07

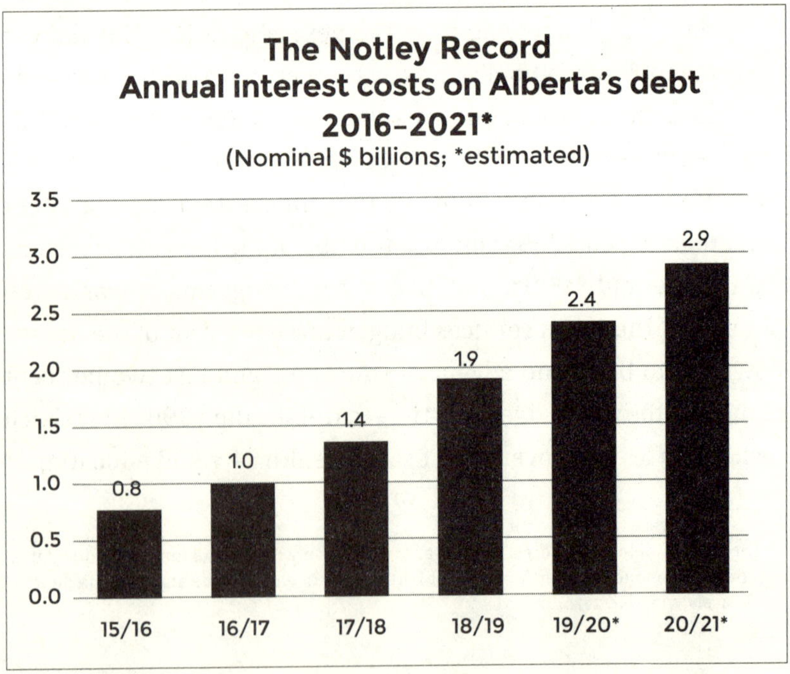
The Notley Record
Annual interest costs on Alberta's debt
2016–2021*
(Nominal $ billions; *estimated)
3.5
3.0
2.5
2.0
1.5
1.0
0.5
0.0
0.8
1.0
1.4
1.9
2.4
2.9
15/16
16/17
17/18
18/19
19/20*
20/21*

NDP SPENDS $750,000 TO ADVERTISE 'THEIR PLAN'...
artizans.com
SPEND LIKE CRAZY...
TAX LIKE MAD!
ALBERTA'S
NDP

8
The flat tax vs. progressive and higher taxes

"Stock, any politician can raise taxes, it's a no-brainer. We have to give people a break. The only way taxes are going is down."

Ralph Klein, to Finance Minister Stockwell Day[1]

"The 1990s are calling and they want their ridiculous ideas back."

Premier Rachel Notley, March 2018[2]

The Alberta Advantage knocks

To uncover a politician's core attitude to voters, here is an acid test: Do they describe tax reductions as a "cost" to the treasury, or reference tax relief as subsidizing the rich (or anyone else)? If so, it means they think income is the default property of governments, instead of the people who earn it, and that tax relief should be as infrequent as Haley's Comet. Ralph Klein made no such mistake. After bringing the budget back into balance, controlling interest costs, paying down debt, and spending out of existing revenues and not more debt, the Klein government moved on another priority that helped create the Alberta Advantage: tax relief. By the early 2000s, that would include a single rate of tax with a generous exemption to make sure no Albertan paid more income tax than under the previous system. Everyone was a winner.

That tax direction—down—was the opposite of much Alberta government policy in most years from Peter Lougheed to Don Getty. Even Klein swallowed a planned rise in business taxes handed to him by the Getty government. That took effect on New Year's Day 1993, just weeks after the Progressive Conservative Party leadership race that Klein won and that catapulted him into the premier's office. It would also be the last major tax increase in the province for over two decades. Thus, after the province's fiscal mess was cleaned up—by the late 1990s—there was room to reduce previous tax hikes, including lowering the general rate and scrapping two high-income surtaxes imposed in the 1980s to fight the deficit. There was also an opportunity to consider the broader question: What type of tax system and levels might encourage economic growth and send Alberta's economy to new heights?

The 1990s and automatic escalator taxes

One reason to revise the provincial tax system was how Alberta, as with other provinces, was locked into a federal-provincial arrangement with provincial income taxes calculated as a portion of federal rates. In 1998, Alberta's personal income tax was "44 per cent"—a rate based not on income but on a percentage of federal tax rates. The link meant that when Ottawa raised its taxes, a provincial tax increase was automatic. In theory, the province could lower its proportion to avoid a double-whammy to provincial taxpayers. In practice, many governments were happy to let their income tax collections rise with federal increases; if "outed," they could always blame it on federal policy. Also, that link meant provincial tax brackets mirrored steeply higher federal tax brackets.

And there was another problem, something called "bracket creep". Taxpayers were pushed into higher tax brackets by inflation. The policy dated from the 1980s and the federal government under Brian Mulroney and then finance minister Michael Wilson, part of a 1980s-era effort to garner extra taxes and lessen budget red ink, with the hope that most Canadians would never notice the stealth tax increase. One remedy to both bracket creep and the automatic rise in provincial taxes was to stop calculating provincial income tax merely as a portion of federal rates. After the federal government agreed to that, made-in-Alberta possibilities were wide open. The start of the path to tax reform came with the 1998 Alberta Tax Review Committee, commissioned to consider changes to the province's personal tax rates, and with a similar committee, to ponder business taxes, a few years later.

Flat taxes from Asia to the Baltics

Later politicians, Rachel Notley included, would portray the single-rate tax as some sort of odd experiment. But it was not revolutionary. When Alberta considered a flat tax,[a] Hong Kong residents had already filed under a simplified flat-tax regime for more than a half-century, since 1947. Multiple American states also did what Alberta proposed, levying just a single tax-rate on income.

---

[a] What is often called a "flat tax" by the public, pundits, and politicians is actually something economists and others refer to as a single tax. In short, the difference is that a true flat-tax system would have no basic personal exemption to shield the first bit of income earned from income tax. It would be a bad idea, given that the poor and everyone else would immediately be taxed on their first dollar earned. Instead, most tax systems, including so-called flat-tax systems, have a personal exemption and one rate of tax—one "flat" rate, thus the reference to a flat tax. In technical terms, it is a single-rate system: A basic exemption and one tax rate.

Two California academics, Robert E. Hall and Alvin Rabushka, trumpeted the idea of federal flat-tax in 1981 on the editorial page of the *Wall Street Journal*. Their later book called *The Flat Tax*, published in 1985, contained a postcard-sized tax form as a visible example of what they aimed for: simplicity. The Hall-Rabushka plan won editorial endorsements from both the liberal *New York Times* and the conservative *Wall Street Journal*. Both Republicans and Democrats introduced bills for Washington to enact a flat tax, though the movement was eclipsed when U.S. President Ronald Reagan signed the *Tax Reform Act* in 1986, replacing multiple tax brackets and a top tax rate of 50 per cent with two rates of 15 per cent and 28 per cent.

After the fall of the Berlin Wall in 1989, an impetus for flat taxes came from nations forcibly incorporated into the Soviet Union or under Soviet rule in the Warsaw Pact. After the 1989 revolutions and the subsequent disintegration of the U.S.S.R., countries in the region began to adopt the flat tax to simplify collection, encourage compliance, attract investment, raise wages, create jobs, and in general help alight formerly struggling economies. Multiple eastern and central European countries adopted variations of the single tax system, starting with Estonia in 1994 and Latvia and Lithuania in 1995, with 12 more to follow.

When Alberta adopted the flat tax, it was thus not a new idea or restricted to one political party—even in Canada. In 1990, former Liberal member of parliament Dennis Mills proposed a 25 per cent rate;[3] the Reform Party similarly endorsed the idea in 1992 and again in 1996 without committing to a specific rate.[4] In advance of the 2000 federal election, the Canadian Alliance proposed the "17% Solution," a single tax-rate of 17 per cent but that maintained all federal tax deductions, credits, and loopholes. After Alberta's single tax, the Fraser Institute endorsed a flat tax in at least two full reports over the years,[5] while Maxime Bernier, before he was Canada's foreign affairs minister, proposed a flat 20-per-cent-tax rate while employed at the Montreal Economic Institute in 2003.[6]

Enter Alberta

While a more comprehensive flat tax (and which would require federal cooperation) would scrape the tax system free of loopholes, credits, and deductions, the Alberta version was modest: one tax rate instead of multiple provincial tax brackets. Also, so long as the province implemented a generous personal exemption, a system could be created that lowered the tax take for all. In the 1998 deliberations of which I was part as then Alberta director of the Canadian Taxpayers Federation (CTF), including in our report titled "Simpler, Lower, Flatter," the CTF endorsed the idea of a single rate of tax with a generous personal exemption.[7] The result of our efforts and others came to fruition when, in 1999, Alberta Finance Minister Stockwell Day announced that the province would sever the federal-provincial rate structure and move to a flat tax with the most generous personal and spousal exemptions in the country—60 per cent and 90 per cent higher, respectively, than existing exemptions.[8] Under the new system, a single-income family at $30,000 would save $1,775, while a $75,000 single-income family would save $1,166. In announcing the Alberta approach to tax, Day referenced a teacher and a nurse in the legislature visitor's gallery, asking the rhetorical question aimed at the critics across the aisle and outside the legislature, "Why they should not have their burden lifted a little as they prepare for the challenges of the 21st century?"[9]

Canada's first flat tax came into effect one year early, in 2001. The proposed 11-per-cent rate was dropped to 10 per cent and the exemptions moved higher, to $12,000. Combined with previous reductions, the newest tax relief meant Alberta's personal income taxes had been cut on average by 23 per cent. In rolling out the reform, the province trumpeted the progressive nature of the reform. "There are two ways to establish a progressive tax system," said the new finance minister, Steve West, responsible now for its introduction. "One way is to tax high income earners at a very high level, the other is to tax low income earners at a very low level," said the minister. "We decided to take the most compassionate approach and not tax the lowest income earners at all."[10] Indeed, the flat-tax system with its generous exemption had, on New Year's Day 2001, just dropped 200,000 taxpayers from the provincial rolls.

The critics: Taxes are too low

The flat tax attracted critics from the start. In 1998, when the Tax Review Committee announced its recommendation for a single-rate tax, NDP Leader Pam Barrett said it would benefit the wealthy at the expense of the middle class. "A flat tax guarantees that," said Barrett to an *Edmonton Journal* reporter.[11] In 1999, Barrett again repeated the inaccurate charge that the proposed single rate of tax came at the expense of the poor and that the new system was not progressive, e.g., the notion that the more one earns, the greater proportion of that income one should pay in tax. "Progressivity in an income tax system has demonstrated to be the fairest form of taxation and that's why it should be maintained," said Barrett on budget day 1999, when the new system was announced. The heads of organized labour chimed in supporting the NDP leader's script. "I believe some middle-income families will not see any savings at all," said Alberta Federation of Labour president, Audrey Cormack. The president of the Alberta Union of Provincial Employees, Dan MacLennan, portrayed the new system as a sop to the rich. MacLennan argued that he "could not see why higher income earners needed a tax break at all."[12]

An Edmonton economist complained that the poor and wealthier Albertans would receive the largest benefit under the new system. "This would really shift the tax burden to the middle class," said economist Mel McMillan.[13] In 2000, the newest NDP leader targeted the soon-to-be-implemented single tax, arguing that "Under this unfair flat tax, 25 per cent of the total tax cuts flow to the richest one per cent of Albertans," said Raj Pannu. "That is nothing short of obscene."[14] In 2001, in an attempt to spur government union members to the polls, and on the assumption they would recoil against the flat tax and the government, Alberta CUPE President Terry Mutton argued that in past elections, "If more of us had voted, would we have private hospital legislation, skyrocketing electrical rates, underfunded education and the flat tax?"[15] The next NDP leader, Brian Mason, would repeat the charge against the single-rate tax system in public comments during his tenure.[16]

From Barrett to Pannu and on to Mason, the NDP leaders and their sisters in ideological arms ignored salient and available facts. That included how if one did not pay income tax, whether in a single- or multiple-bracket system, it was inevitable that *any* reduction would make a difference only to those who did. Also, the claim that the burden would shift if high marginal tax rates were dropped missed the central point of the reform: *Everyone* who paid income tax would see a reduction. To complain about that was akin to a climber on Mount Everest griping that another expedition member, the one carrying most of the gear up to base camp, was suddenly relieved of more equipment than the hiker who carried little. The gripe missed the point that the fellow heading up the mountain with the biggest backpack already carried more of the weight.

Other early critics of the flat tax made the same mistake, intentional or not, about the proportion and progressivity of the flat-tax system. The myth that the flat tax was not progressive was repeated by reporters, columnists, left-leaning think tanks, government employees' unions, and a succession of NDP leaders. And the myth spread to the party that originally introduced the single tax, the Progressive Conservatives, when, in early 2015, the last Progressive Conservative Premier Jim Prentice ventured the same opinion as Barrett, Pannu, Mason, and Notley, who in her 2015 election platform wrote of how she wanted to "set aside the P.C.s' worst policies." In the orange election manifesto, the newest NDP leader took dead aim at the single-rate tax. Notley wrote of her hope of "returning to a system of progressive income and corporate taxes in Alberta that ask the most fortunate among us to contribute their fair share."[17]

Non-progressive flat taxes and other myths

The NDP's reflexive criticisms of the single tax, which the new government ended in 2015, was misguided. As an example, ponder the critics' oft-expressed notion that the single-rate tax was not progressive. To understand the error, recall that in 2014 the basic provincial personal exemption was $17,787, with income above that taxed at a flat 10 per cent. To keep it simple, ignore possible deductions and credits and consider how someone earning $15,000 paid nothing in provincial income tax, an effective provincial income tax rate of zero. As for income above that level, here is the proportion of income taxed in that year: at $25,000, 2.9 per cent; at $50,000, 6.4 per cent, and at $75,000 and $100,000, 7.6 and 8.2 per cent, respectively. The existence of a basic exemption always meant that the higher the income, the greater proportion of income paid in tax. The flat tax was always progressive.

As for burden-sharing, middle- and high-income Albertans already paid most of the provincial income tax under the flat-tax system. With data from 2014, the last year the single tax-rate was in effect, it turns out that Albertans with higher incomes already paid for most of government while poorer Albertans paid nothing or little. For the 1.7 million Albertans who made less than $50,000 that year, fully half, or 850,000 Albertans, paid no provincial income tax; their incomes were too low. Also, those who earned less than $50,000 made up 57 per cent of all tax filers, earned 20 per cent of all income, and paid just 8 per cent of all provincial income tax. The reality for those with less than $50,000 in come: half received government services for free while the other half paid little in provincial income tax.

The picture changes for those earning $50,000 to $100,000; they accounted for 27 per cent of all tax filers, made 31 per cent of all income, and paid 31 per cent of all provincial income tax. Albertans who made more than $100,000 accounted for 16 per cent of tax filers, earned 49 per cent of the income, and paid 62 per cent of all provincial income tax. Alberta's six-figure tax filers also paid a greater share of all provincial income tax when compared with any other province. In the other nine provinces, the $100,000-plus tax filers made up just 8 per cent of all filers, earned 31 per cent of all income, and paid 52 per cent of all income tax in their provinces, significantly below the proportion in Alberta. Alberta's higher-income earners helped pay a larger share of the province's income tax than did their cohorts in multiple-bracket "progressive" tax systems in the other provinces.

In her 2015 election campaign, Rachel Notley argued for a new fiscal plan "where everyone contributes fairly."[18] Except everyone already did. The numbers back up Ralph Klein's flat-tax "experiment," one that by any measure, including with reference to progressivity, was a success.

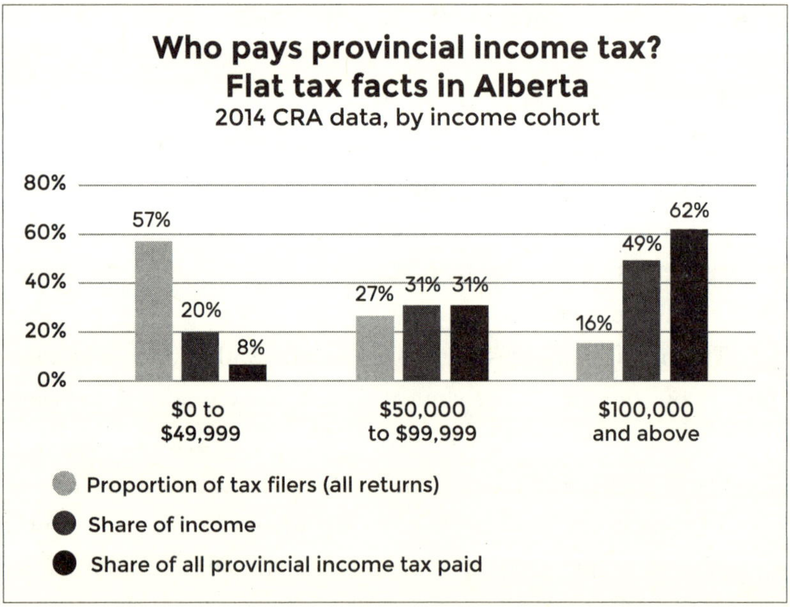

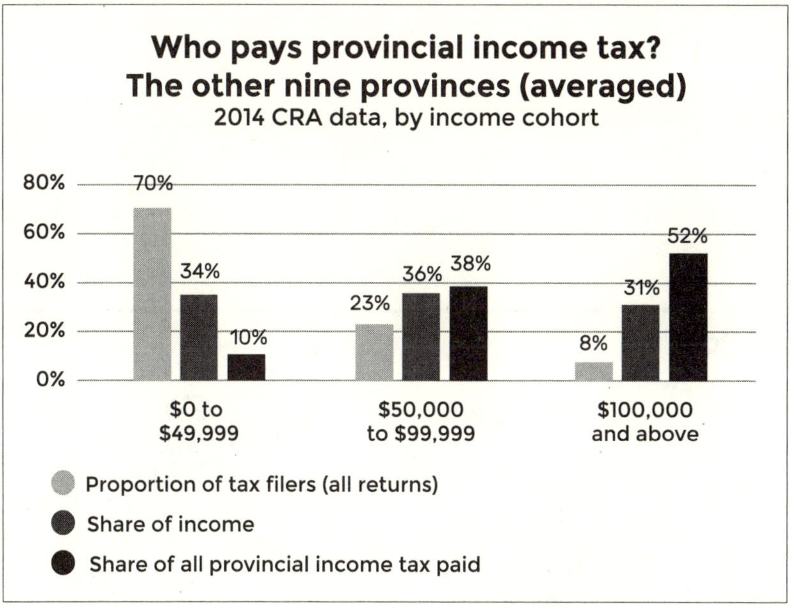
Who pays provincial income tax?
The other nine provinces (averaged)
2014 CRA data, by income cohort
80%
60%
40%
20%
0%
70%
34%
10%
23%
36%
38%
8%
31%
52%
$0 to $49,999
$50,000 to $99,999
$100,000 and above
Proportion of tax filers (all returns)
Share of income
Share of all provincial income tax paid

MAYES edmonton journal
WE'RE SHORT-STAFFED SHORT STAFF.
BOOM CREATES LABOUR SHORTAGE
artizans.com

9

You're welcome: When Alberta rescued Canada's unemployed

"The way to stimulate the economy, corporately and on a personal basis, is to reduce taxes, to leave more money in the pockets of the people, and have more money circulating through the province."

Ralph Klein in his speech to a Montreal business audience, 1994[1]

"Alberta advantage: More Canadians moving here than to any other province."

Calgary Herald headline, July 2005[2]

Opportunity Inc.: Welcome to Alberta

Imagine you are in a troubled marriage, need a divorce, have no money, and also need work but never graduated from high school. In most provinces, you face extremely high unemployment rates and lousy pay because the supply of workers is plentiful. In contrast, in Alberta, a close friend in this situation started her own business, cleaning houses for $35 an hour. The work was hardly glamorous but it served as a bridge until she could return to college to obtain a health-care aide's designation. Later, she worked at what she really loved, caring for seniors.

Opportunities matter and, for two decades, Alberta's pro-opportunity, growth-oriented policies—say "yes" to the province's natural advantages and create a new one, the Alberta Advantage—led to a gusher of new jobs that soaked up legions of unemployed from across Canada. It also drove up incomes, naturally, because businesses were in what seemed like a never-ending competition to find new workers and pay them more to keep them around. And this godsend in employment for many Canadians started with Ralph Klein's economic reforms.

Klein's reforms and early critics

In kicking off the 1997 election campaign, Klein asserted that his government's priority was to create the "climate for growth with... balanced budgets, debt reduction, the lowest overall taxes in Canada and less bureaucratic red tape for industry."[3] Rather than a new direction, it was more a recitation of the existing, deliberate strategy pursued before and after Klein's "Miracle on the Prairies" election win in June 1993: to avoid loading up the private sector with higher bills. Parallel to that were strategies to keep government services vibrant and affordable through competition in delivery, e.g., tendering where possible, or outright privatization as was the case with government liquor store and licence registries.

Then, as now, New Democrats and their ideological allies were critical of not only the Alberta Advantage but what is best described as Ralph Klein's restoration of Alberta's culture of opportunity. To hear the critics of the Klein era today, who range from union executives who should know better to Premier Rachel Notley, the 14 years of the Klein era from December 1992 to December 2006 were ones of unrelenting Dickensian misery with divides and battles between the rich and poor. It is a mythological, foreboding, dark fairy-tale—and voters rejected such claims when they re-elected Klein and his colleagues in 1993, 1997, 2001, and 2004—but New Democrats have always offered up endless versions of this gloomy narrative.

An early example arrived in 1994 with the new Alberta NDP leader, Ross Harvey, who characterized the post-1993 reforms as an attempt "to create a tax haven for large corporations," and claimed this "works against [the government's] stated philosophy of developing economic advantages." Barely one year into the Klein Revolution, as many called it, the NDP leader was sure Klein's policies had failed. He told a Medicine Hat crowd it was a "right-wing economic experiment gone wrong" and "from the point of view of fairness and equity on one hand, and economic common sense on the other."[4] In 1995, Harvey was at it again, stating with certainty that "the policies of this government are not contributing to job growth."[5]

This was predictable rhetoric in the mid-1990s, where the NDP and its allies claimed the Klein era would end in desolation, or already had. As for alternatives, Harvey had earlier (in 1993) advocated federal spending on make-work schemes for roads, bridges, and sewers. Harvey claimed this would create "500 jobs a year for five years in Edmonton alone."[6] In its 1995 convention, the New Democratic Party touted job creation via shorter workweeks (32 hours instead of 40). It was a long-time, left-wing fantasy from Paris to Victoria. Without more money in the economy, or higher productivity, instructing businesses to pay full-time wages for 80 per cent of the needed work did not somehow magically create the ability to pay for new employees for the other 20 per cent. Businesses could not spend money they did not have.

In the 1990s, as Alberta's economy began to speed ahead, the usual suspects were sure that somewhere, somehow, something must be wrong. In 1997 the Alberta Federation of Labour (AFL) released a sour report titled *Crumbs from The Table: Re-evaluating the so-called 'Alberta Advantage'.*[7] In it, the umbrella group for the province's labour unions complained of how jobs in the early 1980s and early 1990s lasted slightly longer in central Canada than in Western Canada. It was telling that the AFL had to reach back to the 1980s—the era of Pierre Trudeau's economically illiterate National Energy Program and which was devastating to the oil patch—or to the early 1990s, and a recession, to complain. Yet here was the AFL carping about the effect of 1980s policy from Ottawa in a document alleging that Klein's policies were mistaken.

Ironically, in its report, the AFL unwittingly gave the real Alberta story in the president's introduction: "1996 was a good year for Alberta. For the sixth time in seven years, our province's economy grew more quickly than the Canadian average," wrote AFL President Audrey Cormack. "The official unemployment rate was one of the lowest in the country. And corporate profits were up for the fourth year in a row. To top things off, the provincial government posted a $2.2-billion surplus - the third multi-million-dollar surplus in as many years."[8] Despite all the positive indicators recounted by Cormack herself, the report grasped for bad news, this to prove Ralph Klein's policies were in the wrong. It was bizarre, but the NDP leader picked up labour's talking points. In 1997, Pam Barrett, parroting the AFL report, said she would create "real jobs" and not "McJobs."[9]

The problem for Harvey, Barrett, and the AFL alike was the economic numbers were not cooperating with their dystopian vision. The same year Barrett claimed no real jobs were being created—and where even the AFL admitted things were great—even the NDP leader had to admit that "the provincial economy is booming." It was just that she claimed to have found fog amidst sunny skies: "Many of the jobs being created are low-wage temporary or casual positions," said Barrett and the NDP in their March 1997 election platform.[10] That was untrue. Alberta's job-creation machine was already chugging along nicely, and the employment created was more full-time than part-time: between January 1993 and December 1996, Alberta's employment numbers shot up by almost 11 per cent. That was double the job creation record in the rest of Canada. Also, 86 per cent of the new jobs in Alberta were full-time compared with just 71 per cent nationwide.[11]

By 1997 the Alberta economy was again described with boom-time references. "Alberta leading new boom," announced the *Calgary Herald* on the front page in late July 1997.[12] In Edmonton, where job creation was also up significantly, the *Edmonton Journal* headlined how "The capital rebounds despite being hard hit by government job cuts." The *Journal's* headline had it backwards, something pointed out by a source interviewed in the article, Allan Warrack. The University of Alberta economics professor, who four years previous was skeptical the government could balance its book through spending reductions, now offered a *mea culpa* of sorts. Warrack pointed out that the elimination of the provincial deficit and cutting the debt helped create about half the capital region's new jobs, care of new private-sector investment. "Governments can really get in the way of progress, so even just getting out of the way helps," said Warrack in response to the journalist's query on the cause of the recovery.[13]

When it was clear that the economy and employment were soaring, Barrett traipsed out a different complaint: Klein was taking credit for jobs created by the private sector, the 157,000 new jobs since 1993. "He's not responsible for them—population growth and private corporations created them," remarked Barrett.[14] Barret never explained how higher population counts necessarily created more employment. Plenty of countries with skyrocketing populations were in abject poverty when Barrett played the demographic and economic expert, but they were hardly job-creating dynamos. The NDP leader also missed Klein's point that permanent private-sector job creation was exactly what the government aimed at since 1993, not make-work projects, as her predecessor had recommended.

Alberta's many years of plenty started in the 1990s

By the end of the 1990s, Alberta was already in a sweet spot: The province's deficit was gone; the provincial debt was in decline; more money was spent on health care and education and less on debt interest; and business investment in the province was increasing rapidly, a critical element in job creation.[15] The latter is often overlooked in commentary on the decade. But when tens of billions of dollars pour into a lightly populated province every year, the effect was akin to the return of rain to mountain lakes after years of drought: downstream rivers fill up and fields become green. In Alberta, business investment by 1998 was double that of 1991,[16] and that created more jobs, higher incomes and a widespread prosperity shared by many existing Albertans and newcomers alike.

That is the actual Klein record, but the current premier is stuck with 1993 and 1997 talking points from previous NDP leaders. "The lie that looking after only the most fortunate helps everyone else has been proved wrong," said Rachel Notley in Calgary one autumn day in 2016, in her state-of-the-province address.[17] It was an attempt to portray previous opportunity-friendly tax policy as a sop to the rich. (Notley also offered up revisionist anti-factual history and a straw man: Who actually advocates for "looking after the most fortunate"?) Her finance minister tried a more positive approach: to argue for the government's own economic record. In January 2018, when Statistics Canada reported that Alberta gained 26,000 jobs in the previous month,[18] Joe Ceci asserted that this was hopeful evidence and proof that his government's policies were working: "We are going to continue doing the things we've done," wrote Ceci in a Facebook post.[19]

The Klein and Notley job creation records: Summer to summer

The finance minister's January 2018 boast and resolution is a useful starting point for a comparison of the Ralph Klein and Rachel Notley governments and their respective job creation numbers, using the first three years for each premier as the contrast. Begin with July 1993 for Klein, given the June election win that year was Klein's first as premier, and here are the results for both leaders.[20] Over three years, employment under the Klein government surged by almost 121,000 jobs—all private sector, with public-sector employment flat.[a] Under Rachel Notley's first three years, total employment rose by just 24,000, nearly 100,000 fewer jobs than Klein achieved, and with a far different mix. Under Premier Notley, 54,000 private-sector jobs vanished while government and public-sector employment rose by 37,000 (with self-employment higher by 42,000).[21] The Klein record is even more impressive given that the population of Alberta in 1996 was 2.7 million compared with 4.3 million people in 2018.

[a] Numbers are rounded to the nearest thousand. Of note, in Alberta, roughly 90 per cent of public-sector employment is provincial and municipal, with 10 per cent employed by the federal government.

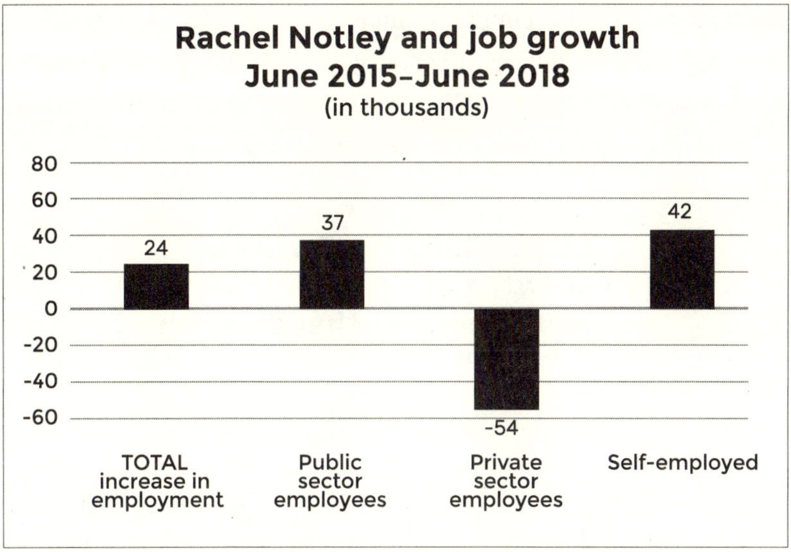

The complete Klein record: Private-sector and public-sector job growth

Beyond any three-year Klein-Notley comparisons, consider Alberta relative to other provinces for Ralph Klein's entire tenure as premier: Alberta's employment numbers grew by 662,000, or 52 per cent, between 1993 and 2006. That was almost double the 27-per-cent increase in the other nine provinces. Under Klein, even the public sector did better relative to the rest of the country. After the initial reductions in Alberta's public-sector job numbers, in the first several years of Ralph Klein's government, public sector employment then thrived relative to the rest of the country.[22] The increase in such employment under Klein was 25 per cent compared to an average *ten-per-cent* increase in the other nine provinces.[23] Klein's budget reforms, which placed the budget on a sustainable track, meant Alberta could hire many more public sector workers relative to other provinces. Alberta's government employees' unions, such as the Alberta Union of Provincial Employees, CUPE, and others should post Klein's picture on their union hall walls.

Ralph Klein: The full record
Job growth between 1993 and 2006
Alberta and the other provinces

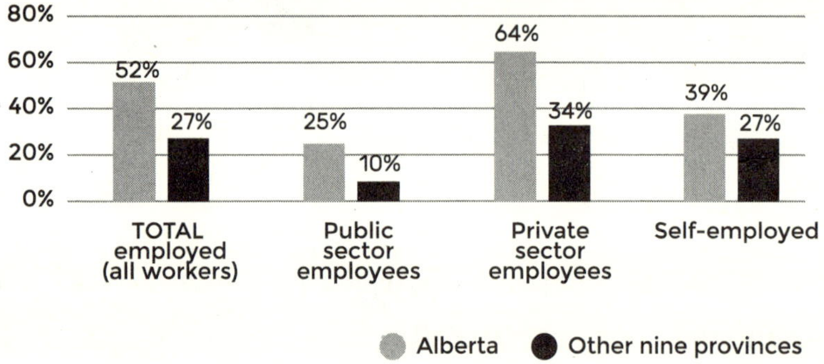

Another Klein accomplishment: Jobs for the least educated

Alberta was a magnet for workers in the Klein years. Between 1993 and 2006, Alberta gained nearly 305,000 people in net migration from other provinces. Only warm-weather British Columbia also recorded net in-migration, with 122,000 people moving to that province. Every other province lost people to Alberta and, to a lesser degree, British Columbia. That included Saskatchewan and Manitoba (over 76,000 and 68,000, respectively), while Quebec lost the most, with 142,000 residents headed west.[24]

Unlike British Columbia, other Canadians arrived in Alberta not for the balmy weather but because the Klein-era policies worked; they attracted investment that led to an overflow of jobs where almost anyone from any background and education level could find employment more easily than in any other province. In Klein's fourteen years, those without a high school education faced an unemployment rate of 10.7 per cent compared to 16.5 per cent on average in other provinces, with Newfoundland and Labrador as high as 25 per cent.[25] The average unemployment rate at other education levels was also dramatically below other provinces and despite the massive inflow of people into Alberta. Back to my soon-to-be-divorced friend, she who would have had a much slimmer chance to find a job and pay her bills in central Canada, other Prairie Provinces, and the Atlantic provinces. She thrived in Alberta, as did many others. That was the true Miracle on the Prairie, how Klein-era reforms led to robust job growth and rescued many of Canada's unemployed.[26]

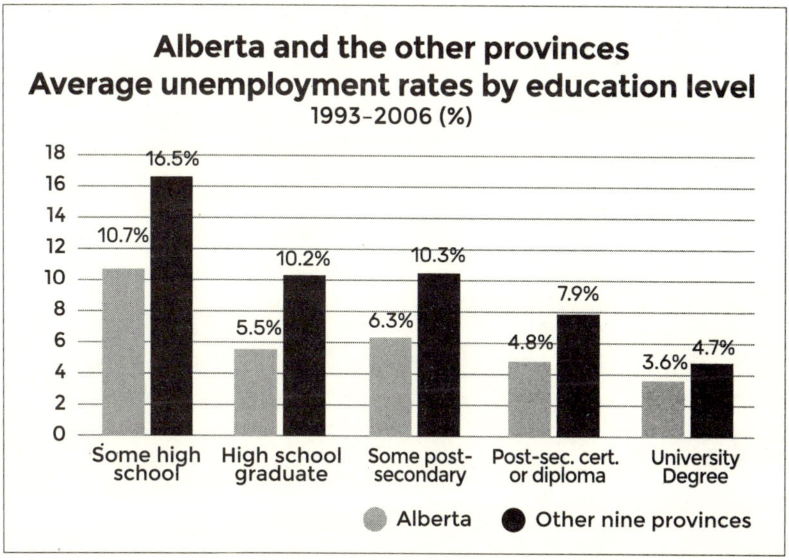

artizans.com
MAYES
edmonton journal
ALTA. NEST EGG
SCRAMBLED OR OVER EASY?
SURPLUS SPENDING

10

Heritage Fund–friendly: Peter Lougheed *and* Ralph Klein

"For far too many years, [previous governments] squandered our resource revenues instead of saving them."

Alberta NDP Finance Minister Joe Ceci, in Budget 2015[1]

Over the next three years, $5.5 billion from year-end surpluses, and non-renewable resource revenue will be reallocated to the Capital Account, Heritage Fund, the new advanced education endowment, and the Medical Research Endowment Fund.

Budget 2005, announcing new fund deposits[2]

My, what big savings funds you have

One enduring myth is that if only Albertans would tax themselves more, as with those responsible Norwegians, Alberta would be awash in a Heritage Fund that might rival Norway's oil-based Pension Fund Global ($1.3 trillion) or at least Alaska's version ($76 billion). Instead, the critics complain, given that successive Alberta governments with rare exception kept moderate tax rates, Albertans possess a fund worth a mere $17.4 billion.[3] Another myth: That Ralph Klein was among those premiers who deposited nothing into the Heritage Fund.

The NDP under Premier Rachel Notley often lobbed such claims at their conservative opponents; but the accusations were best crystallized by Quebecer Brian Topp, a future chief of staff, before the NDP's 2015 election win. Topp, a lifelong New Democrat who ran for the leadership of the federal New Democratic Party in 2012 but lost to Thomas Mulcair, had plenty of advice for Albertans about their money and their Heritage Fund. In a *Globe and Mail* column in 2012, Topp made the Norway comparison and then donned the hero cape, Defender of the Fund. He invoked a popular former Alberta premier and conflated his accomplishments with the wish of a contemporaneous Saskatchewan NDP premier: "Peter Lougheed and Allan Blakeney proposed similar funds for western Canada," wrote Topp in his column. He then accused Lougheed's "conservative successors" of throwing away "a once-in-history opportunity to capitalize on an advanced, diversified economy, in order to pretend we have an 'advantage.'"[4]

Topp's argument was a pastiche of peripatetic points and unrelated factoids.[a] Silly was Topp's attempt to criticize Alberta premiers, considering the province at least *had* a resource fund while Allan Blakeney's Saskatchewan never did. That had everything to do with how Saskatchewan's Co-operative Commonwealth Federation (CCF) and New Democratic Party governments nationalized large swaths of the province's industries. From 1944 and the election of the CCF and Premier Tommy Douglas and beyond, that province's anti-free-enterprise parties nationalized businesses and chased capital from the province and sunk Saskatchewan's fortunes. It led to decades-long stagnation, and it took 60 years, in the case of the

---

[a] I have some familiarity with Peter Lougheed's views on the Heritage Fund as he wrote the foreword my 2006 study on the fund published by the Alberta Chambers of Commerce.

Saskatchewan NDP, to make peace with business.

That peace offering was signalled in the early 2000s when Saskatchewan's social democrats reduced some corporate (and personal) taxes. But New Democrats never declared a détente with free enterprise, nor grasped the proper role of government: To do what markets cannot, not to inhibit investment, employment and prosperity by nationalizing some enterprises and micro-managing the rest. But New Democrats were self-held hostages to their ideological assumption that theorized that if only profit was removed from the balance sheet, then workers could be paid more and consumers charged less with everyone the beneficiary.

It was make-believe economics. It ignored how government Crowns were slow-moving political entities with no reason to innovate and every incentive to be inefficient: No possibility of bankruptcy due to competitive forces, nor any great reward for innovation, as governments do not behave as do institutional or individual shareholders, who send constant signals via share prices. The other problem with government Crowns in sectors where the private sector would normally operate—telephones, power, insurance—is how their presence made it impossible for substantial capital to flow into a province such as Saskatchewan. The potential for profit allows for a province's natural advantages to flourish, attracts investment dollars and boosts economies; it leads to higher employment as well as creativity and innovation. At the end of the economic train, it also creates higher tax revenues than would otherwise exist.

Instead, the NDP's historic capturing of large parts of Saskatchewan's economy, prompted by the ideological fiction of efficient government ownership and effective government delivery, doomed Saskatchewan for decades. Make-believe economics chased money, talent, businesses, and jobs to Alberta. It is why Allan Blakeney could never start a resource savings fund during his premiership: the proclivities of his party anchored his province in mostly what the government itself could "invest" in major sectors of the economy. That historic and antagonistic approach to free enterprise, by preferring government ownership of the commanding heights of the Prairie economy, led to sub-standard economic growth for over half a century. It left little from which any government could divert revenues.

The long-term deleterious effects of anti-free-enterprise economics in Saskatchewan never stopped Premier Rachel Notley, Finance Minister Joe Ceci, or Notley's chief of staff from advancing the claim that conservative-tagged politicians in Alberta blew it on resource revenues. In October 2015, in his first budget speech, Finance Minister Joe Ceci complained that, "For far too many years, they [previous governments] squandered our resource revenues instead of saving them."[5] Ceci's tears were part crocodile—a party that fiercely criticized Klein over the years for not spending enough was now annoyed that the "piggy bank" was nearly empty. Except, as Ceci well knew, resource revenues flow into the same general revenue pot with all other taxes. *Ergo*, one way to build up Alberta's various provincial savings funds over the years was to spend less. More prudence on the spending side of provincial budgets would have created fiscal room for Heritage Fund deposits. That was what Klein did after he became premier and which laid the foundation for significant deposits into three Alberta savings funds, including the most well-known: the Alberta Heritage Savings Trust Fund.

Another option, as the tax-more New Democrats prefer, was northern European–like, to raise taxes on Albertans yet again. But the problem, beyond suppressing incomes in Alberta even more, is this: No necessary link exists between higher taxes and deposits into the Heritage Fund. In the late 1980s, the provincial government under Don Getty *did* tax Albertans more. That new money never went to the Heritage Fund. Instead, in 1987, just as the tax increases started, Getty cancelled all deposits into Peter Lougheed's original rainy-day project: Every extra dollar from new and higher taxes went to government spending and interest on the provincial debt. More recently, the Notley government already raised taxes substantially.[6] None of that extra revenue is headed to the Heritage Fund for future generations. Sometimes a new and higher tax is just a new and higher tax.

A short history of a swell idea

The Alberta Heritage Savings Trust Fund was the creation of Peter Lougheed's government who framed the need for it in a legislature speech in 1976: "Are we prepared as a province to put aside substantial sums of current revenues from the sale of non-replaceable crude oil production?" remarked the premier, "for the sake of our children and for our grandchildren and not make it available for current revenue needs; to use it for that day... when some of the wells may have gone dry?" The enabling legislation was approved in 1976, with the intent to divert a portion of resource revenues to the Heritage Fund every year. In theory, the Heritage Fund could provide options for Albertans and their future governments. Dividend cheques could be sent to citizens every year from some of the fund's investment returns, as took place later in Alaska where its Alaska Permanent Fund issued annual cheques to state residents (US$2,072 per Alaskan, for example, in 2015).[7] Another option: Build up the Fund and over time replace resource revenue streams to the provincial treasury. That was the option chosen in Alberta, the "rainy day" fund.

Soon after the Lougheed government created the Heritage Fund, two deposits were made, one to kick-start it and another based on resource revenues—30 per cent, annually, to be deposited into the fund. That latter practice continued until 1987, though in ever-smaller proportions. After that, deposits ceased for nearly two decades until resumed briefly under premiers Ralph Klein and then Ed Stelmach. By 2018, the fund's market value was $17.4 billion.[8] In comparison, the Alaska Permanent Fund, created the same year as Alberta's Heritage Fund but which accepted its first deposit one year later, was worth $76 billion as of 2018.[9]

There was no great secret to the Alaska fund's growth. By 1976, after the state government spent all the resource revenues from earlier years—"frittered away," how one account of the Permanent Fund describes it[10]—the Alaska legislature responded by crafting a constitutional amendment for voters to approve or deny, to divert 25 per cent of oil revenues to the proposed fund. Also useful was how the Alaska government was prevented in that amendment from touching the fund principal—ever. In November 1976, voters approved that amendment by a two-to-one margin. Four years later, in a fit of good sense, state politicians also passed legislation that required 50 per cent of all newer royalties and other energy-derived income be sent to the Alaska Permanent Fund. As a result of those constitutional and legal safeguards, the state resource fund was guaranteed more deposits and protected from political pillaging. In Alberta, no such voter or constitutional protections existed.[11] In practice, Alberta's Heritage Fund has, in most years, served as just another stream of revenue for the provincial treasury. Arguably, that made it easier for successive governments to overspend when resource booms were in full swing.

Alberta is not a nation-state

Alaska's fund is the one most similar to Alberta and the one to which most reasonable comparisons are made. However, oil-rich Norway, and its initially named Petroleum Fund (now Pension Fund Global) is also occasionally contrasted with Alberta's version. The Norway fund was created much later, in 1990, and, as with the Alberta and Alaska versions, the goal is to divert oil revenues to future generations and their governments. Former federal deputy finance minister Don Drummond cited Norway in 2005, when he recommended that the province forego any further reduction in taxes with its overflowing provincial treasury. He expressed particular concern that Alberta, with gushing energy revenues at the time, might eliminate personal or business taxes and affect the ability of other provinces to compete. To ward off a too-competitive Alberta on tax rates—Drummond's worry but not everyone's—he instead suggested more resource revenues be directed to the Heritage Fund.[12] The former civil servant, unlike other advocates for the Norway model, at least did not recommend higher taxes. More often the Alberta-Norway comparison is made with reference to Norway's higher taxes, with the recommendation, implicit or explicit, that if only Albertans taxed themselves more and relied on resource revenues less, Alberta's Heritage Fund could one day rival Norway's.

The Alberta-as-Norway comparison skips over multiple differences between that Nordic state and a Western Canadian province, which make the comparison faulty. One is that in Norway there is no equivalent of "Alberta," i.e., a major sub-national jurisdiction between the local level and the federal government. In Norway, all resource revenues flow to the national government and then on into its resource fund, just as in Alberta, the resource bounty ends up in the provincial treasury, and on occasion, in the Heritage Fund. But that is where the similarities end. The critical difference is that most other taxes *also* flow to Norway's national government—84 per cent, with regional and local governments taking in what is left. In Canada, the provinces, on average, take in just 40 per cent of all revenues (with the federal and local governments raking in 50 per cent and 10 per cent of all revenues, respectively).[13] In other words, Alberta's proportion of possible revenues will always be smaller than that available to Norway's national government. Alberta has two "competitors" for taxpayer dollars, the federal government and local governments—not just one as in Norway. It is why Norway's national government could more easily build up its national resource fund: With access to 84 per cent of all revenues in the country, the national government could afford to fund higher deposits.

$36 billion to zero: Premiers compared

Faulty national to subnational comparisons aside, the premier with the original idea for a resource fund, Peter Lougheed, was disciplined *and* lucky. His government set aside a significant portion of resource revenues, when oil prices were high and government spending initially modest. However, it was also Lougheed's government that substantially raised expenditures far beyond what population growth and inflation required. That set up his successor, Don Getty, for near-guaranteed failure, given the one-two punch of high spending plus a dramatic swoon in revenues after 1986. Nevertheless, over ten years $35.7 billion was deposited into the Fund.[b] In comparison, Don Getty's government made just one deposit of $460 million, in 1987. Fund deposits resumed under Ralph Klein's government,[14] but only after it balanced the books, restarted much government spending, offered tax relief, and paid off the provincial debt.

The Klein government also created and built up two other funds, the Capital Account and the Sustainability Fund, started in 2003 and 2004, respectively.[15] Deposits were anything but modest, with nearly $16.4 billion, and which served as the province's de facto rainy-day funds.[16] Klein received little credit, then or now in comparison to Peter Lougheed but for all three funds, the Klein government's contributions totalled just over $20 billion, with his successor's government, led by Ed Stelmach, depositing $4.6 billion. The record: Klein and post-Klein governments built up three savings vehicles, with $24.6 billion in diverted revenue in just six years.

In contrast, the NDP government, which chose to spend more and delay a balanced budget, will deposit nothing into any savings fund in its first term in office nor in its second should it be re-elected, given that a balanced budget is delayed until at least 2023. And

---

[b] As per my practice in this book, the year here refers to the fiscal year that ends on March 31 (i.e., "1985/86" is "1986,"), and I give each premier credit for the years in which they were mostly in office. When a deposit was made in the year ending March 31, 2007 (i.e., 2007), Klein is credited given he served nine months in that fiscal year. The fund figures are adjusted for inflation to 2018 dollars.

despite billions in new taxes since 2015, the province spent it all and deposited not a dime into Peter Lougheed's legacy. In practice, after three years in power, the NDP finance minister acted as did (some) previous finance ministers, whom Ceci cheekily criticized in his first budget speech. He squandered resource revenues.

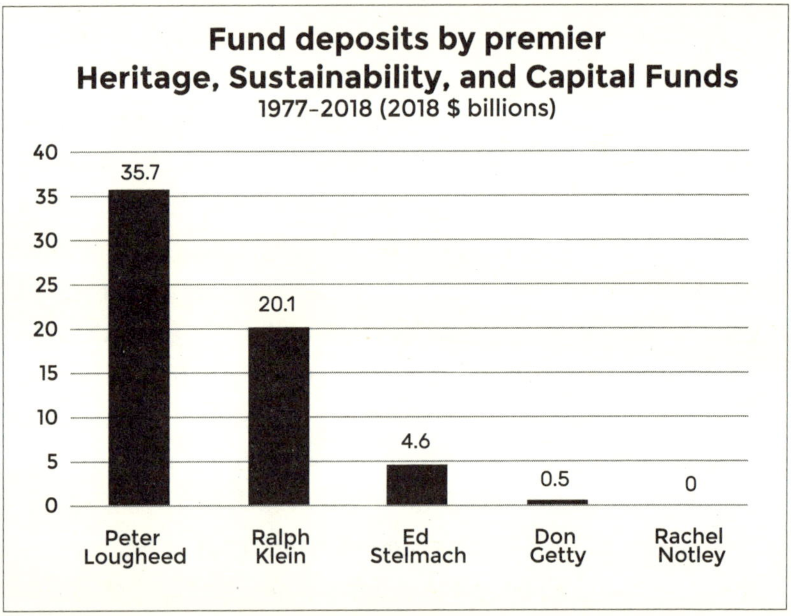

Ralph Klein and $38 billion in capital spending

In the 1990s and for years afterwards, one critique of the provincial government was that while the province turned the budget deficit into a surplus and eliminated the provincial debt, spending on infrastructure was less than ideal.

In Alberta, government spending on schools, roads, hospitals, and other capital projects was cut from $737 per person in 1994 to $481 per person by 1997, after which spending ratcheted higher until 2002, when the province scaled back. A large part of the reason was the decline in oil and natural gas prices (and a subsequent 40 per cent decline in provincial resource revenues), in the fall of 2001, just after the 9/11 terrorist attacks.

Did the Klein government spend enough on infrastructure? The question is impossible to answer. With infrastructure as with much else government can spend dollars on, the "proper" amount is a matter of continual debate and competing priorities. In total, the record is that the Klein government spent $38 billion on capital projects between 1994 and 2007, and also, as described in this chapter, initiated a fund for capital projects from which subsequent governments could spend on infrastructure.

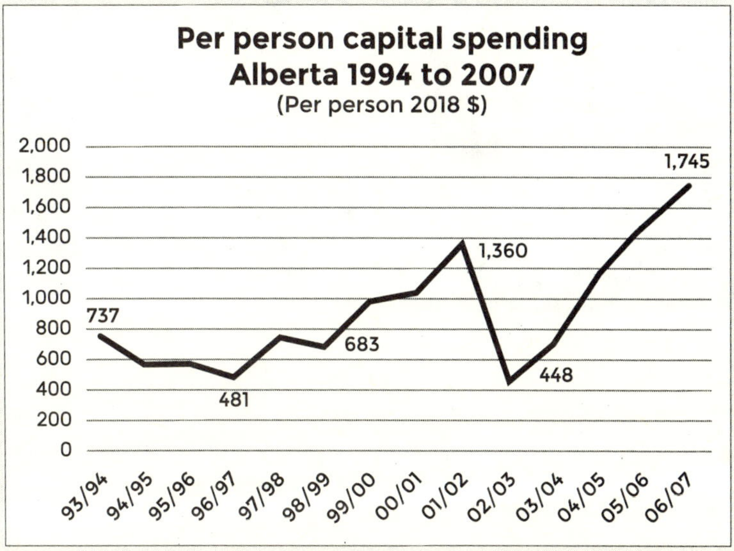

King Ralph...
MAYES
edmonton journal
artizans.com

11

The Alberta Advantage: It wasn't luck

"Unlike some others, my government will not try to buy prosperity through higher taxes. Instead, it will build on Alberta's existing advantage of low taxes and its free enterprise spirit to develop the most competitive economy in North America. The government will strengthen the Alberta Advantage and sell it aggressively around the globe."

Ralph Klein, August 31, 1993[1]

The difference between Alberta and other provinces: Not luck

When Ralph Klein's critics are confronted by his 14-year success story and positive results that extended beyond his 14 years in office, they will finally settle on this explanation: It was all luck—all of it: The job boom; balanced books; elimination of the provincial debt; higher incomes; health-care, education, and social programs financed out of today's revenues and not tomorrow's government credit card; tax relief; opportunities for the poor and those with less education who flourished in Alberta to a degree unknown in any other province; and tens of billions of dollars deposited into provincial savings funds.

All of it. Just luck.

Alberta's success over decades is thus waved away with the notion that, *sure, perhaps all of that is true*, but any village idiot of a province could reap such benefits with oil and gas deep in the earth. And there is a second add-on assumption: How hard is it to extract black gold and gas from nature anyway? Drill, put a pipe down, pump out the black stuff, or scrape away sand, boil some water, and ship it away and see the cheques roll in as if one were J.R. Ewing in some 1980s Dallas episode. This, according to more than a few armchair observers, is the explanation for Alberta's past fortunes, including the occasional healthy state of Alberta's economy and government finances.

It should be self-evident that oil and gas in a province, if not developed, or tourism on a remote island in the South Pacific that lacks airplane access, or any number of natural advantages for any spot of land, are not, on their own, sufficient to create prosperity. Relative to Alberta, government policies, including those in Edmonton, Victoria, Ottawa, and even Washington D.C., matter. The notion that Klein's government was merely a recipient of pixie-dust good fortune (which explained his government's financial success) or the belief that the Notley government is a mere victim of economic forces (about which it can do nothing) both miss the obvious—that prosperity is never automatic. It results from conscious choices by governments and others to lay foundations that allow citizens to entrepreneurially exploit whatever natural bounties exist, be it oil and gas in Western Canada, a geographic proximity to major population markets such as exists for central Canada vis-à-vis the American northeast, or hot weather in Hawaii. But to grasp why the "Alberta was/is lucky" assertion is additionally hollow, consider that other provinces have had rich resources and said no to development. Let us begin with Quebec.

Provinces that say no

The first producing oil well in Canada was drilled not in Alberta but in Enniskillen, in southwest Ontario, in 1858, by James Williams;[2] in Quebec, exploration for oil occurred soon after, in the 1860s.[3] Ontario's petroleum sector was small relative to what would later be discovered in Alberta, but Quebec's oil and gas resource-wealth was left mostly undisturbed then and, more recently, when that province could have chosen a different path. For example, in 2011, the Quebec finance department estimated that the potential for natural gas in the province was between $38 billion and $178 billion in production value. While Quebec's shale-gas sector would be smaller than Alberta's, it would still be substantial enough to make a difference to revenues and jobs, with $2 billion and 11,000 jobs added to Quebec's economy.[4] Similarly, in Atlantic Canada, while Newfoundland and Labrador allowed for offshore oil development and reaped the benefits over the decades, even that province, and Nova Scotia and New Brunswick, banned onshore exploration for natural gas in the past decade. In so doing, all three provinces said no to "luck," to the new employment and additional revenues for governments. In the case of New Brunswick, before it banned onshore exploration, the province estimated it possessed a 350-year in-province supply.[5] When current politicians or others look back to the Klein era and think that the jobs, incomes, and tax and royalty revenues came from nature's good fortune and nothing else, they ignore how political decisions allowed a natural advantage to flourish. The contrary examples exist in Atlantic Canada and Quebec.

A tale of two resource-rich territories: Alberta and Argentina

Have-not provinces such as Quebec and in the Maritimes that reject prosperity are one "proof" that potential resource riches mean little if left unexplored, not extracted and never exported. Another is an example that contrasts with Alberta (and Canada more generally) and also serves as a caveat: A once-prosperous, resource-rich country became relatively poor after politicians chose policies that hampered its economy for decades. Consider the negative example of Argentina, the country known for the tango, beef, and a combination of European-style culture combined with Latin verve.

I first visited Argentina in 2013 and marvelled at its people and potential, its obvious past success as demonstrated in ornate, late-19th- and early-20th-century architecture that rival anything spotted in Paris or London from the same period. At present, though, Argentina is a mixture of past First World glories, a large underclass, and a shrinking middle-class under multiple threats, including continuing high inflation, corruption, crime, and crumbling infrastructure. When I walked around its capital city, Buenos Aires, the beauty and brokenness were both evident with new towers but fragmented sidewalks and a creaky subway system that seemed not to have been upgraded since the 1970s. In Buenos Aires, it was obvious that the governments, businesses, and most citizens often lacked the money to pay for even the civic basics. The cracked sidewalks I spotted in San Telmo, Palermo, and Recoleta—and these were the more affluent neighbourhoods—were an object lesson in how politicians and lousy policy can harm even countries with every reason to prosper and which once did.

In Argentina, some economic problems result from recent decades, including inflation and sovereign debt-defaults, but others originate with political choices made decades before that and demonstrate why the comparison with Canada is relevant: The South American nation was not always a troubled country. In 1900, Argentina's per-capita GDP at $5,051 was *higher* than Canada's at $4,924.[6] As we shall soon see, the numbers today are no longer anywhere near even.

Argentina's decline cannot be explained by a lack of people or a lack of natural resources. Argentina has nearly 45 million people, 97 per cent of whom are literate. Argentina, as with Canada, possesses a plethora of potential wealth creation that matches Canada's: manufacturing, oil and gas resources, mineral wealth, agriculture, and a financial sector—all ripe with the potential for significantly more investment in the last 70 years and today. But Argentina performed far below its historic potential in most of those decades. That has everything to do with the choices made by the country's politicians since the 1940s.

Argentina, cursed by politics

Starting with the presidency of General Juan Domingo Perón, who along with his wife Evita became fixtures of Argentinean social and political life for three decades, Perón would serve as president three times between the 1940s and the 1970s, with Argentina's decline attributable to his policies. The Perónists, as his party and government would be known, were influenced by the fascist and corporatist policies that Perón first observed in Italy under Benito Mussolini, where he was stationed as a military attaché between 1939 and 1941 and where he imbibed many of his flawed economic ideas. The future president was taken with the notion that communism could be held at bay if a government intervened and sorted out disputes between competing groups, a sort of "knocking heads together" approach. As New York banker Eduardo Singerman described Perón's views in a 2015 retrospective, "Perón viewed fascist corporatism as a useful method of social organization by which socially harmonious class participation would lead to a fair distribution of national output, and elude in this way the class warfare predicted by Marxist socialism."[7] Or as historian Adrian Lyttelton and chronicler of Italian fascism described it, "Fascism claimed to have reconciled capital and labour within the so-called corporate state."[8]

If fascism seems like an odd choice to examine in a book about a Canadian government from the interventionist left, the parallel is not in the ideological motivation but in the means employed by both the interventionist left and the Peronist model, in the extreme intervention that characterizes both ideologies. For Argentina, all organizations, whether trade unions, corporations, professional organizations, and special interests, would be subordinated to the state. In theory, because all such organizations and interests would be subordinate to government, the political system could then even-handedly decide, through negotiation or arbitration or decree, how to "balance" the competing interests. For example, in a dispute between a corporation and its trade union, both parties would in theory then be placed—forced really—into always negotiating through government.

In practice, such daily direct intervention meant that government and the politicians who ran it became the final arbiter between multiple private interests and their disputes. Such power-induced "co-operation" between labour and business led to state-favoured monopolies and quasi-monopolies over open competition. It also led to a centralization of even more power in government; corporatism through fascism made the government and politicians the pinnacle of a society's interactions. That political approach made the state nearly all-powerful and to which unions, businesses, and every other interest would always seek to influence, legally or through corruption.[a] Or as an Italian academic wrote, "The sphere of fascism is that of power and not that of profit."[9] It was thus inevitable, as Lord Acton famously observed, that "power tends to corrupt and absolute power corrupts absolutely"[10] or, in this case, that near-absolute power in Argentina corrupted an otherwise decent, prosperous nation from the 1940s forward.

Beyond the problem of overly centralized authority in such matters, which invites civil society to enmesh itself with the state and gives more control to the state, inflating the power of those in office, Argentina under Perón's first presidency engaged in multiple other actions that further wrecked what had been a relatively prosperous, open economy and country before his presidency. Before Perón, Argentina was more akin to Great Britain in its free market heyday, or Hong Kong now, than to what we now call "banana republics."[11] Destructive Peronist policies included nationalization of the central bank, which would lead to both inflationary policy and

---

[a] This is in contrast to Canada, where a business or union negotiates directly and one or both suffer the consequences if a poor agreement is reached. If a union is unreasonable in wage demands, or its employer unreasonably stubborn, the company may end up bankrupt and both the shareholders and employees suffer. It serves as a warning sign to others to engage in reasonable behaviour that the market can afford or similarly perish. Governments in Canada occasionally demand a company and union enter into arbitration, but that is the exception, not the rule.

also to economic favouritism among potential borrowers. Perón's government also set up a ministry to tightly control imports and exports, another feature of not only fascism but its parallel economic error of autarky, or economic nationalism, which sees imports as "stealing jobs" and export sectors as creating them. (It helps to think of Juan Perón as a 1940s version of Donald Trump.) In fact, such policy eventually raises prices and dampens demand, leading to inflation plus high unemployment.

Argentina's decline was directly related to its departure from policies friendly to free enterprise, including; neutrality among businesses and sectors; restraints on unnecessary intervention; and free trade with the rest of the word among other helpful policies. Instead, Argentina's rush into economic populism and corporatism was "populist" interventionism, as opposed to clear left-wing mangling of the economy, but it was a distinction without a difference. Both varieties prove disastrous for foreign investment, growth in the domestic economy, employment, inflation in many instances, and also in depressed revenues to government. For Argentina, Peronism did not solve but instead exacerbated inequality and poverty (just as similar "Chavismo" economics from Hugo Chavez would do the same in the early 21st century to Venezuela). Even worse was how such interventions were constitutionalized, making necessary, systematic, and comprehensive reform in future decades nearly impossible.

Over seven decades, Argentineans were repeatedly subjected to politicians whose penchant for intervention had a direct, negative effect on the market's ability to function properly. While the country under then-president Carlos Menem introduced some sensible reforms in the 1990s—privatization of money-losing state companies and freed-up controls on exports, for example—the country was again ruled by modern-day Perónists Nestor Kirchner (president from 2003 until his death in 2007) and then his wife, Christine Fernandez de Kirchner (president from 2007 until 2015). Both engaged in illiberal politics and interventionist ways reminiscent of the worst of the Peronist years. From Perón onward, Argentina's policies invited chronic rent-seeking by business and labour instead of entrepreneurial openness; economic cronyism and corruption instead of entrepreneurs; a path that ultimately led to economic decline instead of widespread prosperity. The country, even under Mauricio Macri, a more market-friendly president since 2015, is still trying to recover.

Any province or country can poison its own economic well

Which brings us back to how economies prosper. Alberta's "luck" whether in 1947 when a major oil field was discovered at Leduc, or in subsequent decades elsewhere, could only properly flourish in conjunction with a stable, predictable regime: of respect for property rights; light regulation; intervention as the exception and not the rule; supportive legislation in general but neutrality between competing firms and sectors; reasonable tax rates; and an attention to core responsibilities of government but not extraneous diversions. It included the province's protection (until the 1970s and again recently) in the framework of a confederation and a federal government that, until recently, was stable vis-à-vis Alberta and in its own regulatory regime, in protected property rights, and which did not enact excessive and unreasonable hurdles. Until recently in Alberta and the rest of Canada, few desired to mimic third-world governments run by erratic populists or autocrats where investments, property, and money are subject to the whim of their pet theories or utopian ends, and which have little connections to realities on the ground.

That has now changed though for reasons very different from early or mid-20th-century ideologies. Barriers to extracting and shipping Alberta's most valuable commodities were first intentionally obstructed by American-funded anti-energy activists, the Keystone XL pipeline the first notable example, and which became a cause célèbre for the most intransigent environmental groups starting in the later 2000s, akin to activism against forestry in earlier decades. Their cause was taken up by Barack Obama once he entered the White House in 2009 and who successfully blocked that pipeline for two terms. Alberta's economy has also been hampered by domestic federal politicians. They include a Montreal mayor who railed against the proposed Energy East pipeline. It includes Christy Clark who, as then premier of British Columbia in 2012 and desperate to win an election, threw Alberta and the energy sector "under the bus" when she laid down five conditions for the Northern Gateway pipeline.[12] The practical effect was to impede a cross-provincial project and set an example for other premiers. Predictably, two years later, in 2014, Quebec Premier Philippe Couillard and Ontario Premier Kathleen Wynne set seven conditions for TransCanada Corp.'s Energy East pipeline to be allowed to cross "their" provinces on the way to New Brunswick.[13]

Anti-energy advocacy based on a purist notion of carbon elimination that demands not gradual reductions and but swift and imposed, is not restricted to outside Alberta activists. Alberta's New

Democrats have been part of the problem. Consider a sampling: David Eggen, the future NDP education minister, told a 2008 rally in front of the legislature that Alberta's oil-sands development was "poisoning the land, poisoning the water, killing the people." Eggen remarked that "doing the right thing means we have no new approvals for tar sands projects."[14] In 2011, future NDP MLA Robyn Luff showed up at an anti-Keystone XL protest at the main federal government building in Calgary with the sign, "No More Dirty Oil."[15] In 2013, with reference to the oil sands that she despised, future environment minister Shannon Phillips told a Ottawa conference that "You rip it out, ship it out in its rawest form, extracting as little value as you can... as quickly as possible because time is running out politically and ecologically."[16] Brian Mason, the future transportation minister in the Notley government whose pre-political career was to drive a bus fuelled by diesel, also chimed in with this comment in 2013: "The oilsands has [sic] given Alberta and Canada a black eye with the rest of the world."[17] At the time, Mason was leader of the New Democrats.

Rachel Notley also shares some blame for the escalating anti-energy rhetoric that contributed to the poisoned discourse about Alberta cross-country and internationally. In 2008, six months after her first election to the legislature as a New Democrat MLA, the future premier was quoted by a Fort McMurray newspaper with words that could have come from anti-oil-sands advocates, whether Neil Young, Leonardo DiCaprio, Greenpeace, or Tzeporah Berman: "The NDP wants what most Albertans want," said Notley, seven years before reaching the premier's office, "for the Tories to stop issuing new Tar Sands [sic] development leases."[18] In October 2010, after ducks died in an oil-sands tailing pond near Fort McMurray, the NDP

MLA appeared at a Sierra Club rally to decry what she described as "unbridled industrial growth."[19] Over the years, and after becoming premier, Notley also consistently refused to advocate for either the Northern Gateway pipeline or Keystone XL; the NDP leader always believed exports of oil should be minimized in favour of more expensive refining in Alberta, a position kept after she became premier, except relative to the Trans Mountain pipeline.[20] Canada's New Democrats, including in Alberta, have routinely embraced protectionism, autarky, and anti-free-trade positions since their party's inception. They only recently added opposition to a natural Canadian advantage, opposition derived from a romantic, purist notion of the environment that brooks little compromise or any recognition of trade-offs. That Alberta's NDP modified its position in power reveals more about the mainstream of Alberta political culture than about the late conversion to fighting for one pipeline, Trans Mountain. In sum, whether before or after winning power in 2015, there was little difference between anti-energy activists outside Alberta and some MLAs in Rachel Notley's Alberta NDP caucus, including the premier.

Politics can hurt

The presence of resources explains almost nothing about Alberta's prosperity or that of any other modern economy. Prosperity and economic success have less to do with what natural or other advantages exist—oil and gas, massive population cohorts nearby central Canada, a harbour in Hong Kong, or a country with every advantage such as Argentina—than what a specific government does with such realities. Argentina had every advantage that Alberta possesses. Politics is what repeatedly harmed that nation. Alberta has multiple advantages still. Politics—the kind that over-intervenes or sacrifices a natural bounty to the priorities of politicians and activists outside the province—repeatedly harms Alberta. It also injures the "luck" possible in other resource-rich regions be they in northern British Columbia, Quebec or Atlantic Canada.

Back to South America: For all of Canada's overly interventionist policies in some post-war years, especially under Pierre Trudeau, the historical data shows a divergence between the Canadian and Argentine economies since the 1940s, about when Argentina started down its Peronist path. In 1936, before the Second World War, when Canada was still recovering from the Great Depression, Argentinians were still nearly as wealthy, income-wise, as Canadians, with per capita income of $6,872 per person—barely $100 less than the $6,976 figure per person in Canada, and barely more than a one-per-cent difference. Eighty years later, in 2016, per-capita income in Argentina stood at $18,875, with Canadians at $43,745, or 130 per cent higher than Argentineans. Countries and provinces with a great potential for prosperity can both be hurt by politicians who wield harmful policy.

Politics can help

Albertans and Ralph Klein were not lucky. They both chose policies that allowed the province's natural advantages to flourish. Albertans and Ralph did choose *each* other; if there was any luck in Alberta in recent decades, it started right there.

BUILDING
MARRIAGE
DRIVER'S
SOCIAL
PERMIT
NO.
Marriage Certificate
Operators Licence
No. 999902-2
Class 5
Notley, Rachel
Sex: F
MAYES
edmonton journal
artizans.com
GUESS which licence cost us billion$ to obtain?

Addendum A
New Democrats vs. free enterprise

"The NDP's broad goal is to reshape Alberta society and economics."

Columnist and Rachel Notley biographer, Don Braid, in 2016[1]

NDP assumptions: The collectivist bent

In politics, move beyond the importance of voters, friends, family, or the media and social media—each of them important "influencers" on why politicians and governments act in some fashion—and what is left is the powerful tug of an ideology at work. At the heart of the New Democratic Party is a worldview that sees politics and the use of power as the preferred rather than rare, limited option. A default preference for intervention is central to the party's history and how its activists view the world. It is shared by many progressives but is more dominant in the NDP and was also deeply rooted in its predecessor party, the Co-operative Commonwealth Federation.

It helps explain a chronic desire to micromanage the economy and relationships between parents, kids, and teachers, and even try to upend market economies. Progressives and socialists have never suffered from slowness or doubt about their means or aims: The New Jerusalem must be built and we shall do it in haste.

Progressive ideas in early motion

At the founding of CCF, in Calgary, in 1932, the party demanded extreme government intervention as remedy for economic crisis that was the Great Depression. The reaction to the Depression was understandable in sentiment but not in its prescription. The CCF's program was, root and branch, to create a "new" economic system. Proponents assumed that a largely government-owned, government-run economy would function better than the one they blamed for the devastation they observed in the 1930s: grinding, widespread poverty; the lack of a social safety net; the near-absence of what today citizens properly take for granted, such as pensions, selected social welfare supports, unemployment insurance, and universal health-care coverage.

To agitate for those latter instruments of public policy—a net in part paid for by taxation—was one matter and in most cases reasonable. Where the CCF and its offshoot party later erred was in another part of their program. That plan of political action included nationalization of entire industries such as banking; natural resources, including oil, forestry and mines; transportation, including railways and, later, airline companies; electricity; and insurance companies. The CCF saw almost any major economic sector as needing to be subsumed into government.

The reasoning: "What we seek is a proper collective organization of our economic resources such as will make possible a much greater degree of leisure and a much richer individual life for every citizen," noted the Regina Manifesto, the CCF program adopted at its first annual convention, in Regina, in July 1933.[2]

The means: The program and party did emphasize opposition to violence and any attempt to introduce such central planning through anti-democratic means. Most CCFers were not 1917 Bolsheviks and instead believed that this "social and economic transformation can be brought about by political action"—by politics, in other words.

Winning at democratic politics is what allowed the CCF and then NDP governments, over successive decades until the 1970s, to carry out a program of extreme intervention, to nationalize significant portions of the economy in Saskatchewan and Manitoba and, to a lesser degree, in British Columbia. Failed targets included mining and forestry firms, while successful government takeovers included insurance, telephone, and transportation companies, among others.

As with many early- to late-20th-century socialist experiments, the CCF and later NDP platforms assumed central planning: government "direction" on market matters, from prices to the "right" wage. The planners enthralled with their own abilities and persuaded of their own virtue assumed much could be directed from politicians and civil servants.

A Mesopotamian farmer meets a fisherman and...

Except that the 20th century would repeatedly puncture the notion that a basic human activity—trade between peoples had existed since the first fisherman bartered with the first farmer on some ancient Mesopotamian shore—was better managed by technocrats. Or that such voluntary interactions between diverse peoples with differing priorities and interests, and signalled via prices, could be replaced by central planning.

But in liberal democracies, government failure was always easier to mask than private-sector failure. Taxpayers or public borrowing could be used to make up for Crown losses and for a very long time. Also, consumers forced to deal with nationalized sectors had no options. As with much in politics, once implemented, a policy that is also connected to a powerful interest is difficult to dislodge. The rule that special interests often trump the general interest applied to once-nationalized companies. An inefficient Crown corporation with multiple thousands of unionized public-sector employees who have a direct interest in the status quo (paycheque and a job) is difficult to reform. The millions of consumers who pay more under a public-sector monopoly (or who suffer from a lack of innovation) have only a small interest (perhaps several or tens of dollars a month extra). The most direct interest almost always wins. And what was a mid-century Saskatchewan farmer unhappy with the "public" (i.e., government-owned telephone service) to do? Switch to only mail?

It was only in the 1980s when state-owned companies needed obvious replenishment of capital stock (Canadian National Railway) or diverted increasingly large sums of money from the public treasury (coal mines in Great Britain) that privatization occurred. It was a reversal to the historic norm: the private sector would run itself, and governments would tax and regulate as needed.

New Democrats seem to have accepted that latter political reality at present, but they have never dropped the progressive temptation to over-intervene. Moreover, they appear still wary of free enterprise. These days, akin to crusty old preachers who quote less from the Old Testament and now more from the New

Testament, the Alberta NDP's 2016 constitution replaced the anti-capitalist fire-and-brimstone rhetoric against capitalism with a few updated, softer phrases.

They include "the application of democracy to the economy"—code for politically directed government interference in consumer or business choices. The NDP constitution also decries the ability or wisdom of individuals, families, and entrepreneurs to make proper decisions themselves. Instead, the spectre of "private interests" is invoked, as are "transnational corporations." The language is designed to stir up, almost conspiracy-like, images of cabals that control us all. The following excerpt is from the 2016 Alberta NDP constitution:

> Socialism is essentially the application of democracy to the economy. Economic democracy, i.e. democratic socialism, assures production to supply the needs of all people. Decisions about what shall be produced, when and where, and decisions about where we shall make our living and under what conditions, are now left largely in the hands of private interests.
>
> The market economy produces transnational corporations, who give private profit priority over public interest, social justice and workplace democracy. Through the efforts of many, we have achieved a degree of social and political democracy. Economic democracy demands a co-operative rather than a competitive system.
>
> – Constitution of the Alberta New Democratic Party, June 2016

The federal New Democratic Party is also antagonistic to free enterprise. (See the following excerpt from its constitution).

> That the production and distribution of goods and services shall be directed to meeting the social and individual needs of people within a sustainable environment and economy and not to the making of profit; To modify and control the operations of the monopolistic productive and distributive organizations through economic and social planning. Towards these ends and where necessary, the extension of the principle of social ownership....[4]
>
> – Constitution of the New Democratic Party (federal), 2003

Profit, competition, and the organic operation of the marketplace are all considered problematic by its authors. The old-fashioned CCF language about the "proper collective organization of our economic resources" has been replaced with other language, such as "modify and control" and "economic and social planning" and "social ownership."

Be specific: Who exactly should make decisions?

Consider the vagueness of the terms. Only specific entities—an individual, shareholders, a non-profit board, or a government—can own or run something; vague "social owners" cannot. The term "social" or "social owners" seem oddly similar to the equally opaque notion of "society." As the American economist Thomas Sowell once wrote, "There is no one 'society' who decides anything."[5] Or Margaret Thatcher, in a 1987 interview, who remarked that "there is no such thing as society," a common-sense observation for which some pilloried the British prime minister.[6]

Both Sowell and Thatcher meant what should be obvious: No institution known as "society" decides anything. Instead, specific people or institutions with a decision-making structure do: parents, a teacher, a student, a judge, a company board after a vote, and so forth. For observers of politics, or voters, it helps to press those who offer up vague notions on what they mean by "distributive organizations" or "social ownership" or "social licence" (not in the NDP constitution but often used in rhetoric). In practice, such phrases are allusions to old-fashioned collective ownership, control through government or through those sanctioned by government. They are usually political allies of those in power, who are given power, and then often override actual public preferences. It is invasive interventionism in updated language.

New Democrats, whether in Alberta or federal, still see open economies, price signals, economic competition, and voluntary transactions as a blight on human progress rather than an aid. Their interventionist urge has never disappeared. The NDP still decry the market economy even though the rejection of starkly interventionist governments, starting in the 1980s and until recent years, delivered a plunge in absolute poverty rates worldwide, from 44 per cent in 1981 to just 11 per cent by 2013.[7] That occurred after more politicians adopted policies friendly to individuals and not producers, to consumers and not government-owned or government-sanctioned cartels, to entrepreneurs and not nationalized companies—to citizens, in other words, capable of adult choices in open markets in an open world.

Addendum B
Your heroes explain you

"Attacks, harassment and intimidation of those critical of government policies, including journalists and human rights defenders, were widespread."

Amnesty International, on Venezuela and its regime, in 2010[8]

Bizarre hero-worship

Just before Alberta's New Democrats won power in May 2015, Thomas Lukaszuk, the Alison Redford–era cabinet minister, tweeted that he recalled seeing Rachel Notley with a Che Guevara wristwatch.[9] A later online picture confirmed his tweet. Lukaszuk would go down to defeat two days later in his Edmonton riding, but the premier's ideological fashion choice was revealing.

Che Guevara, referred to as simply "Che" for those with a celebrity-style fascination with him, was the mid-century, Argentine communist revolutionary. He served in Fidel Castro's guerrilla army in the late 1950s, and his self-awarded "job description" included executing suspected traitors and deserters or just those who bent the rules of the revolutionary cause. In one case, after a child in Guevara's guerilla unit stole food, the boy was immediately shot.[10] Later, after Castro ousted Cuban dictator Fulgencio Batista, Guevara served in Havana's La Cabaña prison, where "enemies of the revolution"[11] were put to death. They included former Castro's co-belligerents who also hated Batista but disdained Castro's Marxism and instead wanted a return to Cuba's 1940 constitution and liberal democracy. Che Guevara was described by a Bolivian comrade as "an authoritarian through and through" and by a French author as "dogmatic, cold and intolerant."[12] Writing in *The Black Book of Communism* in 1999, Pascal Fontaine described Guevara as "a Latin American version of Nechaev, the nineteenth-century nihilist terrorist who inspired Dostoevsky's *The Devils*."[13]

Che Guevara's image is a common enough visage. In the five decades after his death at the hands of the Bolivian army in 1967, his face is standard fare on wall posters hung by undergraduates intoxicated with some romantic notion of revolution. That is unfortunate enough, but the wristwatch revealed something about a 50-something political leader in the richest province in Canada, where earnings and opportunities in the past century came not from the ideas of a young, violent Latin American hothead, but from the grounded approach to people, power, and the economy worked out over centuries in Great Britain and her offshoots: free peoples, free enterprise, in free societies.

But Rachel Notley chose Che Guevara.

If the premier possessed an odd choice in a wristwatch, she was not alone in her accidentally revealed autocrat preferences. The 2015 NDP election win washed in few others hostile to free enterprise, including Rod Loyola. Pre-politics, Loyola, a union and NDP organizer, habitually praised Hugo Chavez.[14] Chavez, who ruled from 1999 until his death, exacerbated Venezuela's typical Latin American problems—poverty, corruption, graft, and inefficiency—with assaults on institutions necessary for a free society: the media, opposition parties, an independent judiciary, and non-government organizations. He turned a second-world country with promise into a bankrupt, failed state.

An example of Chavez's economic policies: In 2010, the Venezuelan leader launched an "economic war on the bourgeoisie owners" of food distribution chains, flour mills, and grocery stores.[15] His war and the substitution of government agencies for private-sector distribution led to tragic waste. That same year, a state-owned subsidiary failed to transport food from the docks. The result was 80,000 tonnes of rotting food, including meat. The ensuing stench was described as akin to "100 dead dogs."[16]

In 2013, when Chavez died, Loyola was listed by the *Marxist Leninist Daily* as the media contact for an Edmonton "tribute to Chavez." Organizers called on "the Edmonton community to attend this Mass/Tribute/Homage to President Hugo Chávez." Loyola wrote of how it was an "opportunity to express solidarity [and] ... also share with the media and local community, the hard work, dedication and achievements of President Hugo Chávez and his government."[17]

The Notley-Guevara, Loyola-Chavez sympathies are notable, not because one expects the premier or Loyola, who chairs Alberta's standing committee on resource stewardship, to one day hire Latin American revolutionaries to run Alberta's prisons or to nationalize Alberta's energy sector, though, in the 2014 leadership race, Loyola did like the idea of 60-per-cent royalty rates.[18] The sympathies matter because, whether Guevara or Chavez, New Democrats still seemed impressed by revolutionary rhetoric over the hard-work reality of how economies, actual justice, and countries are built and prosper. They still seem entranced, as many New Democrats were in the 20th-century by Mao Zedong, Fidel Castro, and multiple other revolutionaries from Latin America to Africa, with high-sounding ideas and not the actual results under such regimes. It is as if the more ideological New Democrats believe that flipping a rhetorical switch and chattering about social justice can bring about prosperity and actual justice.

Addendum C
Other books on Ralph Klein

"Seventy per cent of the stories on TV were negative when Klein was setting records for popular support."

Political scientists Barry Cooper and Mebs Kanji, in 2000[19]

Ralph Klein and his colleagues made some difficult, overdue choices, in the 1990s and this led to a few books on the premier, some less reasonable than others.

Edmonton Journal Reporter and Columnist Mark Lisac, in his 1995 chronicle *The Klein Revolution,* wrote of how "Meanness was in the air during the early Klein years," though he blamed that more on an "international economy empty of any feeling at all" than on Klein as a person.[20] As with other writers of the period, Lisac would equate government spending with community, and thus any reduction in what a government did was, by definition, anti-community.

Kevin Taft, the academic and later Liberal leader between 2004 and 2008, argued that the entire premise of Klein's reforms was flawed—i.e., that the province could, as of 1993, no longer afford to spend at the same clip. In 1997's *Shredding the Public Interest,* Taft disagreed and argued budget cuts were driven by "greed and ideology," especially on health care, where Taft thought any reductions were just a prelude to privatized health care.[21] Taft painted a dystopian picture of the mid-1990s and Alberta's future.

Peppered among his data were liberally applied accusation-brushes of "cynicism," "manipulation," "lust for glory," "self-interest," a "social unity sacrificed to the politics of divide and conquer," and "a society of haves and have-nots."[22]

Some critics engaged in straw-man assertions and stereotypes that are of little help in assessing Klein's accomplishments or failures. An example comes from Rich Vivone in his 2009 book, *Ralph Could Have Been a Superstar*; Vivone, former publisher of a weekly newsletter on Alberta politics, thought the premier had "swallowed the ideology of business and the ideology of the right: government is the problem, not the solution."[23] While that 1980-era sentiment was famously expressed by Ronald Reagan and captured the zeitgeist of his age (government *was* the problem in the 1970s, when inflation ran rampant and unemployment spiked, with government policy to blame for both), Vivone stretched it when he wrote that such high-level notions were an actual problem. Vivone seemed annoyed that his interpretation of Alberta under Ralph Klein was not shared by most voters.

Not all books on the Klein era were so sour. Journalist Frank Dabbs, a 1960s-era acquaintance of Ralph Klein, wrote the best historical account of the man from childhood to premier. In *Ralph Klein: A Maverick Life*, Dabbs recalls how Klein gave him regular rides in his Volkswagen Beetle when Dabbs was a reporter. He knew Klein "like a cousin or a friendly neighbour," wrote Dabbs.[24] Dabbs wrote, though, of how he spotted the "veniality of power" in Ralph Klein's policies. He alleged Klein "renounced orthodox government without any alternative plan of much detail."[25] Dabbs might have been advised to be more careful about his wish: people and economies are dynamic and too much planning by politicians can interfere in both.

Don Martin's 2002 book, *King Ralph: The Political Life and Success of Ralph Klein*, captured public appreciation for Klein, but even Martin was perplexed that in the mid-1990s Klein's popularity rose when government budgets were cut. "The deeper they cut spending, the higher they rose in the polls," marvelled Martin. He though it an "inexplicable paradox."[26] Elsewhere, Martin noted how Klein exceeded even Peter Lougheed's public approval ratings, with Klein's approval from Albertans at 73 per cent in March 1995, the very time when reductions in government spending were at their deepest inflection.[27] The answer to Martin's astonishment was not mysterious: many voters, after 50 years of post-war government expansion but with increasingly expensive and ineffective government, thought it might be time to reform Leviathan. They were not only on Klein's side but pushed him there.

Writing just five years after that mid-1990s low for spending and high for Klein's poll numbers, political scientists Barry Cooper and Mebs Kanji saw no contradiction in lower spending and higher poll numbers. "It's not rocket science," they wrote in the introduction to *Governing in Post-Deficit Times: Alberta in the Klein Years*. "It is not that Albertans are averse to paying taxes that are reasonable and fair and that constitute payment for essential services and public goods," wrote the authors. "It is, however, irrational to pay taxes and receive nothing in return, which is what debt-servicing charges amount to." Cooper and Kanji argued that many of the accounts written from academia or in the media about the provincial government and its 1990s-era were anchored in assumptions and analyses "conventionally associated with the Left."[28]

The takeaway from Cooper and Kanji: Most Albertans were at core not Pierre Trudeau-type 20th-century social welfare liberals, social justice interventionists, or Prairie socialists, but conservatives or classical liberals. By that they meant that many Albertans believed, acted, and understood instinctively that the best governments for men and women are those that create a framework for civil society but ought not to intervene overmuch in the economy or in our personal lives. They sensed and saw in Ralph Klein a politician who intuitively agreed.

Acknowledgements

While authors no longer hunch over candlelight to complete their work, the creation of what every non-fiction author hopes is a readable volume is a team effort. My deepest "thank-you" to Preston Manning for his foreword and for his service to Alberta and Canada; Faith Farthing at FinalEyes Communications for her editing and proofing; Tiffiny Yaxley for a last-minute fact-check; Jim Davidson for the data on energy prices that go back decades (you saved me countless hours of combing through old Alberta government annual reports); Joel Emes for help with the numbers; Richard John and Patrick Donnelly for reading early versions of the chapters; Charles Adler and Scott Hennig for their read of the chapters and their kind endorsements; Nancy Wise for her business partnership and friendship since Sandhill Books distributed my first book in 2001; Haley Love and Jeff Billingall for their whip-smart marketing help; Milan Szabo for his spectacular layout; cartoonists Malcolm Mayes and John Larter for permission to reprint their work; and Artizans.com for facilitating the same.

Endnotes

Chapter 1: Early NDP temptations

1 CBC News, "Alberta Declares Itself Debt-Free," July 12, 2004, https://bit.ly/2MbMy8r.

2 Jen Gerson, "Former Alberta Premier Ralph Klein Dies at 70," *National Post*, March 20, 2013, https://bit.ly/2Cve3tU.

3 *Hansard*, British Columbia, April 1, 1993.

4 *Hansard*, British Columbia, April 3, 1992.

5 *Hansard*, British Columbia, April 7, 1993.

6 Gordon Jaremko, "Albertans Demand Bite From Sky-High Revenues: 'It's Critical We Get The Best Return ... Today,'" *Calgary Herald*, June 30, 2006, D4.

7 *Calgary Herald*, "Where The Leadership Contenders Stand: The Herald Examines Candidates' Positions On Six Key Policy Issues," *Calgary Herald*, November 25, 2006, A17.

8 Gordon Jaremko.

9 Ibid.

10 Jason Fekete, "Do Albertans Get Fair Share From Oil? Candidates Debate Resource Royalties," *Calgary Herald*, September 17, 2016, A4.

11 Government of Alberta, Annual Report of the Auditor General of Alberta, 2006–2007, Volume 1 of 2, 91, https://bit.ly/2Ql07DM.

12 New Democratic Party of Alberta, Platform 2004: Agenda for Change, 10.

13 Jim Davidson, historical data on natural gas and oil prices (Alberta Natural Gas Reference Price and Western Canada Select), GMP FirstEnergy; correspondence with the author September 18, 2018.

14 Jim Davidson, historical data on natural gas and oil prices (Alberta Natural Gas Reference Price and Western Canada Select), GMP FirstEnergy; correspondence with the author September 18, 2018.

15 Gordon Jaremko.

16 Ibid.

17 Jason Fekete, with files from Kelly Cryderman, "Leadership Hopefuls Back Royalty Review: Morton, Dinning Spar Over The Issue," *Calgary Herald*, November 30, 2016, A4.

18 Jason Fekete and Tony Seskus, "Stelmach Hints Oilpatch Will Get 'Time To Adjust'," *Calgary Herald*, October 25, 2007, A1.

19 Jason Fekete et al., "Stelmach Under Fire: Industry And Opposition Criticize Province's New $1.4B Royalty Hike," *Calgary Herald*, October 26, 2007, A1.

20 Jason Fekete et al., "Premier Stands Firm On Royalty Hikes," *Calgary Herald*, October 27, 2007, A1.

21 Jason Fekete et al., "Stelmach Under Fire; Industry And Opposition Criticize Province's New $1.4B Royalty Hike," *Calgary Herald*, October 26 2007, A1.

22 Jason Fekete et al., "Premier stands firm on royalty hikes."

23 Mark Milke and Mark Rovere, "Have PC Leadership Hopefuls Ever Been to Europe?". *Calgary Herald*, August 21, 2011, A9.

24 Michelle Lang, "Nurses Would Be Highest Paid In Canada With New Contract; Wages Alone Won't Address Staffing Shortage: Union," *Calgary Herald*, June 20, 2007, A4.

25 Government of Alberta, Budget 2012 Speech, https://bit.ly/2QgD8fa.

26 Mark Milke and Milagros Palacios, *Fumbling the Alberta Advantage*, Fraser Institute, February 2015, https://bit.ly/2Lw6nXq.

27 Government of Alberta, "Alberta Focused On Fiscal Restraint," Alberta Finance news release, November 26, 2014, https://bit.ly/2Qfyo9m.

28 Don Braid, "PCs Use OPEC To Build Case For Possible Tax Hike," *Calgary Herald*, November 27, 2014, https://bit.ly/2wTEMdH.

29 CBC News, "Jim Prentice Eyes Public Sector Wages In Budget Crunch," January 21, 2015, https://bit.ly/2CAHlHG.

30 Government of Alberta, Fiscal Plan 2014–17, "Alberta's Progressive Tax System," https://bit.ly/1xDADSY, 120.

31 Government of Alberta, "Alberta's Single Income Tax Rate Lowered to 10 Per Cent," news release, January 3, 2001, https://bit.ly/2NSvZ2i.

32 Ibid.

33 Government of Alberta. *Fiscal Plan 2015-20*. https://bit.ly/19pvEiP. 22–24.

Chapter 2: Similar Economic Storms in 1993 and 2015

1 Joan Crockatt, "Oilpatch On Ropes, Orman Says: Minister Uses 'R' Word To Describe Industry's Troubles," *Edmonton Journal*, February 13, 1992, B16.

2 Chris Varcoe and Darcy Henton, "Tanking Economy Raises Fears: Job Losses, Grim Forecasts Spark Anxiety, Finger-Pointing," *Calgary Herald*, November 19, 2015, A1.

3 Rachel Notley, Twitter, June 16, 2018, https://bit.ly/2OOCQaL.

4 Statistics Canada, Table 36-10-0222-01, "Gross domestic product, expenditure-based, provincial and territorial, annual (x 1,000,000)," https://bit.ly/2oP0LP8.

5 British Columbia, Confidence and Supply Agreement Secretariat, May 30, 2017, https://bit.ly/2NZTVl7.

6 Clare Clancy, "'It Is A Crisis': Alberta Premier Withdraws Support For Federal Climate Plan After Trans Mountain Approval Quashed," *Edmonton Journal*, August 31, 2018.

7 United States Energy Information Administration, "Cushing, OK WTI Spot Price FOB (Dollars per Barrel)," undated, https://bit.ly/2CAzE47; United States Energy Information Administration, "Price of U.S. Natural Gas LNG Imports (Dollars per Thousand Cubic Feet)," undated, https://bit.ly/2wV9PWC; Inflation calculations from Statistics Canada, Table 18-10-0005-01, Consumer Price Index, annual average; TD Economics (June 2018) Provincial Economic Forecast: Forecast Tables.

8 Jim Davidson, historical data on natural gas and oil prices (Alberta Natural Gas Reference Price and Western Canada Select), GMP FirstEnergy; correspondence with the author September 18, 2018

9 Bank of Canada, Bank Rate, undated, https://bit.ly/2CzYLnQ.

10 Bank of Canada, Average Residential Mortgage Lending Rate – 5 Year, undated, https://bit.ly/2oSKWau.

11 Mark Milke, "Alberta's $22-Billion Lost Opportunity: How Spending Beyond Inflation + Population Growth Created Alberta's Red Ink," Fraser Institute, August 16, 2013, 10, https://bit.ly/2MSNT5f.

12 All per-person program figures are from the Department of Finance (federal) Fiscal Reference Tables, 2000 and 2017, and Budget 2018 (Alberta Finance), Fiscal Plan, 156; Inflation calculations from Statistics Canada, Table 18-10-0005-01 "Consumer Price Index, annual average, not seasonally adjusted," https://bit.ly/2MVCvJI; TD Economics (June 2018) Provincial Economic Forecast: Forecast Tables.

13 Mark Milke, "Alberta Tosses Clear Budget Language," *Financial Post*, March 12, 2013, https://bit.ly/2oOAqAV.

Chapter 3: A core NDP belief: Albertans are undertaxed

1 Alberta Federation of Labour, "Let's Face It – Alberta Has a Problem, a Revenue Problem," News release, September 8, 2010, https://bit.ly/2wXOPiA.

2 Mark Lisac, "A Test of Populist Politics," *Edmonton Journal*, May 19, 1993, A1.

3 Government of Canada, Corporate Income Tax Rate Database: Canada and the Provinces, https://bit.ly/2NrA4hr, A5.

4 Elections Alberta, "Candidate Summary of Results (General Elections 1905–2015)," https://bit.ly/2PrTyju.

5 New Democratic Party (Alberta), "We're Fighting Back!" 1997 platform.

6 Graham Thomson, "New Democrats Would Tax The Rich: Platform Includes Five Tax Brackets, Scraps Tax Breaks: Alberta Votes 2001," *Edmonton Journal*, February 16, 2001, A1.

7 New Democratic Party (Alberta), Platform 2004: Agenda for Change, 4.

8 New Democratic Party (Alberta), Platform 2008: On Your Side.

9 Ibid.

10 New Democratic Party (Alberta), Platform 2012: Because Alberta Belongs To You, 18.

11 Ibid.

12 Alberta Federation of Labour.

13 Shannon Stunden Bower, Trevor Harrison, Greg Flanagan, "Stabilizing Alberta's Revenues: A Common Sense Approach," Parkland Institute, February 28, 2013, https://bit.ly/2oSTG0i.

14 New Democratic Party (Alberta), Platform 2015: Alberta's NDP: Leadership for What Matters, 22.

15 Mark Lisac, "Taxing Message a Tough Sell," *Edmonton Journal*, February 6, 1994, A5.

16 *Edmonton Journal*, "Cuts Avoidable, Harvey Says," December 15, 1995, A8.

17 Elections Alberta, Candidate summary of election results, 1905–2015, https://bit.ly/2PrTyju.

18 Alberta, 2015a, June 18, "Legislation Introduced to Restore Fairness to Alberta's Tax System," news release, https://bit.ly/2O2Razz.

19 Ibid.

20 Ibid.

21 Department of Finance (Canada), Fiscal Reference Tables (1996: tables 25 and 34); (2017: tables 26 and 31), https://bit.ly/2Ntgdew.

22 Government of Alberta, Budget 2015 (October), 2015, 85, https://bit.ly/2LBCHbs.

23 Ibid., 6.

24 Ibid., 32.

25 Ibid., 114–115.

26 Ibid., 26.

27 Government of Alberta, Climate Leadership: Report to Minister, November 20, 2015, https://bit.ly/2ztdueJ.

28 These calculations include the offsetting small-business-tax reduction.

29 Government of Alberta, Budget 2016, 5–6, https://bit.ly/2PISIQo.

30 Ibid., 5.

31 Based on the numbers announced in the 2015 and 2016 budgets, here's how the total is arrived at: The tax and fee measures announced in October 2015 are worth $1.5 billion in 2015/16 and $2.3 billion annually in the next three years (I assume $2.3 billion in that final year) and which total $8.5 billion. Carbon tax proceeds announced in 2016 are worth $4 billion over three years.

32 Michelle Bellefontaine, "Alberta Premier Rachel Notley Doesn't Rule Out Future Talks on PST," *CBC News*, April 15, 2016, https://bit.ly/2oOD8GG.

Chapter 4: The first temptation of Rachel Notley: *Meddle*

1 Emily Mertz, "Premier Notley Facing Criticism for 'Taking a Bus' Comment on Carbon Tax Impact," *Global News*, December 16, 2016, https://bit.ly/2MahrKk.

2 Ibid.

3 Chris Varcoe, "'Not Fully Baked' – Alberta Businesses Fret as Carbon Tax Nears," *Calgary Herald*, December 15, 2016, https://bit.ly/2CxZ2HI.

4 Metro Calgary, "NDP Carbon Tax Will Cause Calgary Food Bank to Spend Extra $31,000," June 7, 2016, https://bit.ly/2wWInrp; Mark Milke, "Of Course, Higher Taxes are Killing Jobs and Hurting Charities," *Calgary Herald*, June 11, 2016, https://bit.ly/2Nv5NOT.

5 Licia Corbella, "Workers and Employer Go to Court to Fight Union Trickery and Alberta's New Labour Law,' *Calgary Herald*, February 16, 2018, https://bit.ly/2oSEZuc.

6 Kevin Libin, "Rachel Notley's NDP Gets Gropey with Alberta's Heritage Fund," *Financial Post*, October 18, 2016. https://bit.ly/2MzvNZM; Kevin Libin, "Emails Show Rachel Notley's NDP Meddling Further in the Running of Alberta's Heritage Fund," Financial Post, March 27, 2017; Kevin Libin, "Tension Keeps Rising Over Alberta's Heritage Fund After Another Ambush of Political Tampering from Notley's NDP," *Financial Post*, May 25, 2017, https://bit.ly/2MRvcCf.

7 Government of Alberta, Electricity Quick Card; AESO 2014 Annual Market Statistics.

8 Government of Alberta, Advisory Panel on Coal Communities, undated, https://bit.ly/2CvYrq9.

9 Government of Alberta, "New Transition Supports for Alberta Coal Workers," news release, November 10, 2017, https://bit.ly/2MZBxMK.

10 Grant Morgan, "Alberta to pay three power companies $1.36 billion to shut their coal-fired plants early," *Financial Post*, November 26, 2016, https://bit.ly/2xkfQfL.

11 Keith Gerein, "AHS Bid to Save Millions Denied: NDP Scuttles Plan to Privatize Laundry Service," *Edmonton Journal*, August 17, 2016, A1.

12 *CBC News*, "AHS Laundry Privatization Stopped after Sarah Hoffman Intervenes," August 17, 2016, https://bit.ly/2NXsTe1.

13 Keith Gerein.

[14] Ibid.

[15] CBC News, "Health Minister Cancels $3B Contract, Will Not Expand Private Services in Alberta," August 13, 2015, https://bit.ly/1MmTEmH.

[16] Kim Trynacity, "Total Cost of Cancelling New Private Lab Service Surpasses $4M," *CBC News*, June 18, 2016, https://bit.ly/2wSkgdq.

[17] Jennie Russell and Charlie Rusnell, "Former Alberta Health Services CEO Vickie Kaminski Says She Resigned Due to NDP Political Interference," *CBC News*, April 25, 2016, https://bit.ly/2CwFMKE.

[18] CBC News, "AHS Laundry Privatization Stopped after Sarah Hoffman Intervenes," August 17, 2016, https://bit.ly/2NXsTe1.

[19] Ibid.

[20] Andrea Ross, "Rachel Notley Blasts Opposition in Campaign-Style Speech to Supporters in Edmonton," *CBC News*, March 3, 2018, https://bit.ly/2ws1iu3.

[21] Government of Alberta, Budget 2015, https://bit.ly/2LBCHbs, 34.

[22] Ibid.

[23] Chris Varcoe, "Two-Stepping Inside Alberta's Beer Market," *Calgary Herald*, July 14, 2016, https://bit.ly/2oSHXyI.

[24] Emma Graney, "Trouble Brewin': Premier Notley 'Will Not Be Lectured' on Beer Prices," *Edmonton Journal*, July 19, 2016, https://bit.ly/2oQE7WD.

[25] Much academic work has been done on subsidies to business. I summarized some of the literature in multiple reports written for the Fraser Institute. For a recent study, see Mark Mike, *Government Subsidies in Canada – A $684 Billion Price Tag* (Vancouver: The Fraser Institute, 2014), https://bit.ly/2x2uwkn. For a literature review, see Mark Milke, *Corporate Welfare: A $144 Billion Addiction* (Vancouver: The Fraser Institute, 2007), 27–36, https://bit.ly/2oSJ6Xa.

[26] There are many examples of this, but my favourite story is how the federal government paid for the construction of a new fish-processing facility in Quebec in the 1980s at a cost of $2.2 million. The subsidy was initially justified with reference to 250 new jobs to be created when the plant opened its doors. However, as the auditor general noted a decade later, the nearby existing fish-processing plant (which also received federal subsidies) closed with job losses equivalent to those "created" by the other, newly subsidized facility. Net employment gains were zero because jobs were transferred—not created—at a cost to the public purse. (Source: Charles Lammam, Hugh MacIntyre, Jason Clemens, Milagros Palacios, and Niels Veldhuis, "Federal government failure in Canada," The Fraser Institute, 2013 edition, 59, https://bit.ly/2MkU3dd.

[27] Madame Justice Gillian Marriott. Court of Queen's Bench of Alberta. "Steam Whistle Brewing Inc. v Alberta Gaming and Liquor Commission, 2018 ABQB 476, June 19, 2018. https://bit.ly/2MBYYHU, para 93.

[28] Ibid.

[29] Joe Ceci, "Minister Defends Moves on Beer," *Calgary Sun*, June 14, 2017, A15.

[30] Madame Justice Gillian Marriott, para 92.

[31] Ibid., para 109.

[32] Emma Graney.

Chapter 5: Reality matters: The Ralph Klein approach

1 Joan Crockatt, "Ralph's Reign: Year Two: $700M in Cuts During Year One Are To Be Followed by $900M More in Year Two as the Klein Gov't Expedites Change," *Edmonton Journal*, June 18, 1994, C1.

2 Lou Hyndman, Alberta Finance, Budget Address 1985, March 23, 1985, 12.

3 Ibid., 27.

4 Dick Johnston, Alberta Finance, Budget Address Update 1986, June 16, 1986, 9.

5 Dick Johnston, Alberta Finance, Budget Speech 1987, 13, 25.

6 Don Braid, "Debt Issue Many-Sided," *Calgary Herald*, December 8, 1988, A3.

7 Jeff Adams, "Sales Tax Inevitable, Analyst Warns," *Calgary Herald*, April 16, 1992, D10.

8 Mark Milke, "The Rhetoric and the Reality of Alberta's Deficits in the 1980s, 1990s, and Now" (Vancouver: The Fraser Institute, 2011).

9 Dick Johnston, Alberta Finance, Budget Address 1987, March 20, 1987, 13.

10 Alberta Finance, "Historical Consolidated Fiscal Summary, 1984–85 to 2003–04," Budget 2001 (Fiscal Plan 2001–04), 58, https://bit.ly/2Q6anBN.

11 Dick Johnston, Alberta Finance, Budget Speech 1988, March 24, 1988, 11.

12 Joan Crockatt. "'Revenue Base Ravaged by Petro Dive' – Johnston; Shortfall in Oil, Natural Gas Predictions May Be $700M," *Edmonton Journal*, April 2, 1992, A7.

13 Ibid.

14 Canadian Press, "Johnston Clings to Budget Target," *Calgary Herald*, December 16, 1988, A12.

15 Barry Cooper and Mebs Kanji, *Governing in Post-Deficit Times: Alberta in the Klein Years* (Calgary: University of Calgary: 2000) 48.

16 Quoted by Jim Dinning, Alberta Finance, Budget Address 1993, May 6, 1993, 8.

17 Joan Crockatt, "A Budget for Voters; No New Taxes But Dinning Cuts $703M," *Edmonton Journal*, May 7 1993, A1.

18 *Edmonton Journal*, "Klein Won't Budge on Cuts Despite Weekend Protest," *Edmonton Journal*, October 25, 1993, A5.

19 Rick Pedersen, "Klein's Spending Cuts Go Too Deep, Economists Warn," *Edmonton Journal*, May 29, 1993, A1.

20 Trevor Harrison, "Hatred, Fear of Poor Makes Us Easy Prey for Politicians," *Edmonton Journal*, September 14, 1993, A11.

21 *Calgary Herald*, "Klein Didn't Blink," *Calgary Herald*, January 18, 1994, A4.

22 Lou Hyndman, 29.

23 Dick Johnston, March 24, 1988, 24.

24 Cooper and Kanji, 41.

25 Sheldon Alberts and Dave Pommer, "Deficit Woes Began in '79," *Calgary Herald*, December 11, 1993, A1.

26 Marina Jimenez, "Voters Less Willing to Follow Politicians Blindly – Pollsters: Glib, Slick Style Doesn't Work: People Interested in Specifics," *Edmonton Journal*, May 22, 1993, A7.

27 Canadian Press, "Poll May Have Guided Tories: Sampling Found Canadians Worried About Deficit Over Jobs," *Edmonton Journal*, November 1, 1993, A3.

28 Ibid.

Chapter 6: Klein-era prudence and NDP pump-priming

1 Clyde Farnsworth, "Budget Cuts Paying Off For Premier Of Alberta," *New York Times*, January 1, 1995, https://nyti.ms/2N6PJDL.

2 CBC News, "Alberta's Credit Rating Takes Another Hit, Despite Economic Recovery," November 29, 2017, https://bit.ly/2x4H9dB.

3 New Democratic Party (Alberta), 2015 Platform: Alberta's NDP: Leadership for What Matters, 3.

4 Ibid.

5 An example: In its 2015 platform, the NDP warned "experiments in privatization" would end with money "redirected" back to government services—i.e., anything owned by government, run by government, and staffed by government employees' unions. The flaw in the plan is that public sector monopolies are no more superior to private sector monopolies and arguably worse, given that even private sector monopolies have some accountability to shareholders. However, neither is optimal for the delivery of goods or services. It is why most people comparison-shop for automobiles, food, housing, and much else. Pricing possibilities, quality, and other outcomes are all improved by choice. It is why governments, for construction contracts and automobile leasing, tender bids, to avoid the trap of a solo supplier.

6 Roman Cooney, "Tory Future Would Be Full-Scale Attack on Deficit," *Calgary Herald*, June 11, 1993, A5.

7 New Democratic Party (Alberta), 2015 Platform: Alberta's NDP; Leadership for What Matters, 24.

8 Government of Alberta, Budget 2015 (March), 112, https://bit.ly/2NJ3YhA; Government of Alberta, Budget 2018, 156, https://bit.ly/2NcfB0T.

9 New Democratic Party (Alberta), 2015 Platform: Alberta's NDP; Leadership for What Matters, 24.

10 Government of Alberta, Budget 2015 (October), 4, https://bit.ly/2LBCHbs; Government of Alberta, Budget 2018, 79, https://bit.ly/2NcfB0T.

11 Government of Canada, Fiscal Reference Tables 2017, 33, https://bit.ly/2Ntgdew; Government of Alberta, Budget 2018, "Historical Fiscal Summary," 156, https://bit.ly/2Ntgdew. (Summary calculations by author.)

12 As of 2007, the Progressive Conservatives began to deplete Alberta's financial assets, from $43 billion to just under $14 billion by 2015. That was a $29-billion decline in eight years, and which emptied out much of the Klein-era savings funds.

13 Statistics Canada, Table 36-10-0222-01: Gross domestic product, expenditure-based, provincial and territorial, annual.

Chapter 7: How Ralph Klein saved health care and education

1 *Edmonton Journal*, "For The Record: Provincial Budget '96,'" February 23, 1996, A5.

2 Don Martin, *King Ralph: The Political Life and Success of Ralph Klein* (Vancouver: Key Porter Books, 2002), 23.

3 *Calgary Herald*, "Big Budget Cuts Trigger Outrage Among Unions and Public Interest Groups," February 17, 2015, https://bit.ly/2MbeitD.

4 Paul Martin, Remarks to the MacDonald-Laurier Institute, Ottawa, Ontario, January 2, 2018, https://bit.ly/2Qfdxmy.

5 *Canadian Press*, "Poll May Have Guided Tories: Sampling Found Canadians Worried About Deficit Over Jobs," Edmonton Journal, November 1, 1993, A3.

6 Emma Graney, "Climate Change Initiative Draws Frosty Reaction," *Calgary Herald*, November 18, 2016, A6.

7 Government of Saskatchewan, Budget 2017, 13, https://bit.ly/2NiFexd.

8 Canadian Labour Congress, "Rachel Notley and a Tale of Two Provinces," 28th Constitutional Convention, May 8–12, 2017, https://bit.ly/2x0pAeG.

9 Rachel Notley, Twitter, August 22, 2018, 12:30 p.m.

10 Geoffrey Morgan, "Calgary's Trinidad Drilling Cuts One in Five Salaried Workers, Slashes Capital Spending by 50%," *Financial Post*, February 17, 2015, https://bit.ly/17Ogq7k.

11 Dan Healing, "Trican Cuts Wages, Implements Variable Pay 'To Preserve Jobs,'" *Calgary Herald*, April 13, 2016, B1.

12 Lorne Gunter, "NDP Coddling Civil Servants While the Private Sector Bleeds," *Edmonton Sun*, September 10, 2018, https://bit.ly/2N5qyBj.

Chapter 8: The flat tax *vs.* progressive and higher taxes

1 Stockwell Day, "Ralph Klein Was 'Genuine,' Kept His Word," CBC News, March 20, 2013, https://bit.ly/2ws13PF.

2 Andrea Ross, "Rachel Notley Blasts Opposition in Campaign-Style Speech to Supporters in Edmonton," CBC News, March 3, 2018, https://bit.ly/2ws1iu3.

3 Dennis Mills, *The Single Tax* (Toronto: Hemlock Press, 1990), 87.

4 Julian Beltrame, "Manning Eyes Flat Tax Plan," *Calgary Herald*, January 23, 1996, A5.

5 Joel Emes and Jason Clemens et al., "Flat Tax: Principles and Issues," (Vancouver: Fraser Institute, 2008); Niels Veldhuis and Alvin Rabushka, "A Flat Tax for Canada," (Vancouver: The Fraser Institute, 2001), https://bit.ly/2CzG6IL.

6 Maxime Bernier, *Pour un taux unique d'imposition : Pour en finir avc le mythe des taux progressifs* (Québec (Province): Les Edition Varia, 2003).

7 Mark Milke, "Simpler, Lower, Flatter: A Submission to the Alberta Tax Review Committee" (Edmonton: Canadian Taxpayers Federation, July 14, 1998), https://bit.ly/2wmY0Jf.

8 Stockwell Day, Alberta Finance, Budget Speech 1999: 12–13, https://bit.ly/2MvBVCd.

9 Ibid.

10 Government of Alberta, "Alberta's Single Income Tax Rate Lowered to 10 Per Cent," (Edmonton: Government of Alberta, January 3, 2001), https://bit.ly/2NSvZ2i.

11 Larry Johnsrude, "'Burden' Falls on Middle Class, Economist Says: Flat Tax Winners and Losers," *Edmonton Journal*, October 30, 1998, B3.

12 Jonathan Jenkins, "No Pain, Some Gains," *Calgary Sun*, March 12, 1999, 4.

13 Larry Johnsrude, B3.

14 Journal staff, "Pannu Officially Named ND Leader," *Edmonton Journal*, November 6, 2000, A7.

15 Larry Johnsrude, "Alberta Votes 2001: Campaign 83," *Edmonton Journal*, March 2, 2001, A7.

16 New Democratic Party (Alberta), 2012 Platform: Because Alberta Belongs to You, 5.

17 New Democratic Party (Alberta), 2015 Platform: Alberta's NDP: Leadership for What Matters, 4.

18 Ibid., 5.

Chapter 9:
You're welcome: When Alberta rescued Canada's unemployed

1 Joan Crockatt, "Budget Worth Losing Election Over, Klein Tells Montreal Business Lunch," *Edmonton Journal*, March 1, 1994, A3.

2 Marty Hope, "Alberta advantage: More Canadians moving here than to any other province," *Calgary Herald*, July 23, 2005, J3.

3 Steve Chase, "Klein Targets Job Creation," *Calgary Herald*, February 5, 1997, A1.

4 *Edmonton Journal*, "Conservative Agenda Won't Work, Says NDP," Edmonton Journal, October 28, 1994, B5.

5 Tom Arnold, "Real Estate, Insurance High on Jobless Figures," *Edmonton Journal*, August 5, 1995, A1.

6 Morgan Waters, "Jobless in Riding 23% – Harvey," *Edmonton Journal*, August 11, 1993, B14.

7 Gil McGowan, *Crumbs From The Table: Re-Evaluating the So-called 'Alberta Advantage'*, AFL Research Department, Alberta Federation of Labour, March 1997, https://bit.ly/2PcNE5C.

8 Ibid.

9 New Democratic Party (Alberta), We're Fighting Back! 1997 Platform, 13–14.

10 Ibid.

11 Statistics Canada, Statistics Canada, Table 14-10-0287-01 Labour force characteristics.

12 Eric Beauchesne, "Alberta Leading New Boom," *Calgary Herald*, July 24 1997, A1.

13 Marta Gold, "Jobs: The Capital Rebounds Despite Being Hard Hit By Government Job Cuts," *Edmonton Journal*, February 22, 1997, H1.

14 Steve Chase, "Klein Targets Job Creation," *Calgary Herald*, February 5, 1997, A1.

15 Statistics Canada, Table 36-10-0222-01, Gross domestic product, expenditure-based, provincial and territorial, annual.

16 Ibid.

17 Mark Milke, "Rachel Notley's Latest Attack on Success," *Calgary Herald*, October 22, 2016, A14.

18 Statistics Canada, "Labour Force Survey, December 2017," January 5, 2018, https://bit.ly/2NrHP3U.

19 Joe Ceci, Facebook, January 5, 2018, https://bit.ly/2Pev2lH.

20 My calculations start in the month just after each government was elected and span 37 months—i.e., July 1993 to July 1996 for Ralph Klein and June 2015 to June 2018 for Rachel Notley (June 2018 being the most recent month for available employment data in researching for this book). As with all governments, the assumption is that most substantive reforms begin after an election. However, with a January 1993 to January 1996 analysis, the numbers are as follows: 13,000 job losses in the public sector, with 117,000 job gains in the private sector, including self-employed.

21 Statistics Canada, Table 14-10-0288-01, "Employment by class of worker, monthly, seasonally adjusted."

22 Ibid. The cross-country comparisons examine January 1993 to December 2006, when Klein retired. For a look back at just the first three years, early public-sector job losses in Alberta were not far off the experience of other provinces. The entire public sector shrank by 13,000 jobs between early 1993 and early 1996 in Alberta, a reduction of five per cent, comparable to other provinces where a 3.5-per-cent reduction occurred in public payrolls in those three years.

23 Statistics Canada, Table: 14-10-0288-01 (formerly CANSIM 282-0089), "Employment by class of worker, monthly, seasonally adjusted,"

24 Statistics Canada, Table 051-0012, "Interprovincial migrants, by age group and sex, Canada, provinces and territories, annual (persons)."

25 The unemployment rate for those who never finished high school ranged from 10.6 per cent in Saskatchewan to 24.7 per cent in Newfoundland and Labrador. The nine-province average was 16.5 per cent. Saskatchewan and Manitoba both continually lost residents to Alberta in this period, collectively almost 145,000, which explains their relatively low unemployment rates in some years in some categories. That trend only reversed later in the case of Saskatchewan after the NDP and then the Saskatchewan Party began to enact business-friendly reforms after decades of the opposite policies.

26 Given there were only two years worth of educational and work data available for the Notley years, 2016 and 2017, I did not insert the data into this chapter vis-à-vis the first two Klein years. (I assume neither 1993 nor 2015 can wholly be attributed to either premier's policies. The statistics on unemployment levels relative to education are favourable to Notley only once. The rates for those who never finished high school for Klein's first two years and Notley's: 13 per cent vs. 15.4 per cent; high school, 7.6 per cent vs. 9 per cent; some post-secondary, 8.9 per cent vs. 9.2 per cent; post-secondary certificate or diploma, 7.6 per cent vs. 6.8 per cent (the one statistic that favoured Notley's government); university, 4.9 per cent vs. 6.1 per cent.

Chapter 10: Heritage Fund-friendly: Peter Lougheed *and* Ralph Klein

1 Government of Alberta, Budget 2015 Speech, https://bit.ly/2MXlJcm.

2 Government of Alberta, Budget 2005, "2005–2008 Fiscal Plan," 3, https://bit.ly/2N3Dsz6.

3 According to Norges Bank's "Market Value," the fund was worth 8,337 billion kroner as of June 30, 2018 (https://bit.ly/2t2QLWI). According to Alaska Permanent Fund Corporation, Permanent Fund balance as of June 30, 2018, was US$64.9 billion (https://apfc.org/) (converted to Canadian dollars using Bank of Canada currency converter); Alberta Finance, Alberta Heritage Savings Trust Fund 2017–2018 Annual Report, 2018: 3, https://bit.ly/2wjbA0a.

4 Brian Topp, "Raw Resources: Remembering Our History in Order Not to Repeat It," *Globe and Mail*, May 21, 2012, https://tgam.ca/2wvX30k.

5 Government of Alberta, Budget 2015 Speech, https://bit.ly/2MXlJcm.

6 Government of Alberta, Budget 2015 (October), 114–115, https://bit.ly/2PNB5Pw; Government of Alberta, Budget 2016, 5–6. https://bit.ly/2PISIQo.

7 Alaska Department of Revenue, Permanent Fund Dividend Division, "Summary of Dividend Applications & Payments," 2018, https://bit.ly/2Lr1ejD.

8 Government of Alberta, Alberta Heritage Savings Trust Fund 2017–2018 Annual Report, 2018, 3, https://bit.ly/2wjbA0a.

9 Norges Bank, 2018, Market Value. The fund was worth 8,337 billion kroner as of June 30, 2018, https://bit.ly/2t2QLWI. Alaska Permanent Fund Corporation. 2018. Permanent Fund balance as of June 30, 2018, US$64.9 billion, https://apfc.org/ (conversion to Canadian dollars; Bank of Canada currency converter, Government of Alberta, 2018, Alberta Heritage Savings Trust Fund 2017– 2018 Annual Report, 3, https://bit.ly/2wjbA0a.

10 Jonathan Anderson, "The Alaska Permanent Fund: Politics and Trust," *Public Budgeting & Finance*, Volume 22, Issue 2, Summer 2002, 68, https://doi.org/10.1111/1540-5850.00073.

11 Details on the various funds can be found in several of my reports, as can the links to historic work on the funds. Mark Milke, "Vision 2020: Phase Three. Saving for the Future Alberta Advantage, Alberta Chambers of Commerce," 2006, https://bit.ly/2MRCtlq; Mark Milke and Milagros Palacios, "Fumbling the Alberta Advantage" (Vancouver: The Fraser Institute, 2015) https://bit.ly/2Lw6nXq.

12 Don Drummond, "Alberta Should Go the Norway Way," *Globe and Mail*, August 31, 2005, https://tgam.ca/2MpdhP1.

13 OECD, "Revenue Statistics - OECD countries: Comparative tables, Chapter 4 - Countries - Tax revenue and % of GDP by selected taxes," https://stats.oecd.org/index.aspx?DataSetCode=REV. Comparative figures based on 2016 data from Norway and Canada.

14 Alberta Finance, "Historical Summary of Operations," Alberta Heritage Savings Trust Fund, Annual Report 2018, 21. Inflation calculations: Statistics Canada, Table 18-10-0005-01: Consumer Price Index, annual average, not seasonally adjusted; TD Economics (June 2018) Provincial Economic Forecast: Forecast Tables.

15 The Sustainability Fund and Capital Fund were combined into one entity in 2009/10. To calculate the latter two funds, I credit both Klein and Stelmach with whatever increased value existed in the funds in the years attributed them. The Heritage Fund calculations are straightforward: the actual amounts deposited. All figures are adjusted for inflation to 2018 dollars.

16 Alberta Finance, Government of Alberta 2012–13 Annual Report, https://bit.ly/2oeTk3x. The Sustainability Fund and Capital Fund were combined into one entity in 2009/10. To calculate the latter two funds, I credit both Klein and Stelmach with whatever increased value existed in the funds in the years in which they were in power—in Klein's case, to March 2007, given his December 2006 departure was three quarters through the existing budget year. The Heritage Fund calculations are straightforward: the actual amounts deposited. All figures were adjusted for inflation to 2018 dollars.

Chapter 11: The Alberta Advantage: It wasn't luck

1 Government of Alberta, Hansard, August 31, 1993, 9, https://bit.ly/2PNz5Wt.

2 Fathi Habashi, "The First Oil Well in the World," *Bulletin of Historic Chemistry*, Volume 25, Number 1 (2000), 64, https://bit.ly/2N6lFXX.

3 Canadian Energy Research Institute, "An Assessment of the Economic and Competitive Attributes of Oil and Natural Gas Development in Québec," November 2015, 13.

4 Government of Quebec, "A fair and competitive royalty system for responsible shale gas production," Budget 2011–2012, 8 and 39, https://bit.ly/2MJtpuS.

5 Government of New Brunswick, The New Brunswick Oil and Natural Gas Blueprint, May 2013, https://bit.ly/2C5Xu7R.

6 Inklaar, R., de Jong, H., Bolt, J., & van Zanden, J. L. (2018), "Rebasing 'Maddison': new income comparisons and the shape of long-run economic development," GGDC Research Memorandum, Vol. GD-174 (Groningen: Groningen Growth and Development Center), https://bit.ly/2pke76p.

7 Eduardo Singerman, "Perón's Legacy: Inflation in Argentina, An Institutionalized Fraud," *Forbes*, January 30, 2015, https://bit.ly/2PqX3qa.

8 Adrian Lyttelton, Italian Fascism, in "Walter Laqueur. *Fascism: A Reader's Guide.*" (Berkeley and Los Angeles: University of California Press, 1976), 139.

[9] A. Tasca quoted in Adrian Lyttelton.

[10] Lord Acton, Letter (i) to Mandell Creighton, 1887, https://bit.ly/2LOSvrA.

[11] Natalio R. Botana and Ezequiel Gallo, *Liberal Thought in Argentina* 1837–1940, translated by Ian Barnett, Liberty Fund, 2013.

[12] Christy Clark, "National Energy Strategy Must Address B.C. Pipeline Worries," *Globe and Mail*, July 28, 2012. https://tgam.ca/2Cg2jLA.

[13] Adrian Morrow, "Premiers Wynne and Couillard Set Seven Criteria for Energy East," *Globe and Mail*, November 21, 2014, https://tgam.ca/2ou9Eh9.

[14] David Eggen, "Stop the Tar Sands," You-Tube, March 8, 2008, https://bit.ly/2CSaMoz.

[15] Don Braid, "New Democrats Called the Oilsands 'Dirty' Long Before Obama Did," *Calgary Herald*, November 6, 2015, https://bit.ly/2QveS8S.

[16] Jarrah Hodge, "Women's Forum/Forum Des Femmes Morning," Gender Focus, November 3, 2013, https://bit.ly/2p2VFix.

[17] Jackie L. Larson, "Mulcair's U.S. Visit Leads to Fireworks During Question Period at Alberta Legislature," *Edmonton Sun*, March 19, 2013, https://bit.ly/2MI69gM.

[18] Cited by Lorne Gunter, "NDP Civil War Between Notley and Singh a Minor Skirmish," *Edmonton Sun*, August 15, 2018, https://bit.ly/2xdFgMQ.

[19] Rachel Notley, YouTube, October 20, 2010, https://bit.ly/2PQehxN.

[20] Canadian Press and National Post, "Alberta Premier Sides with Hillary Clinton on Her Opposition to the Keystone XL Pipeline," *National Post*, September 23, 2015, https://bit.ly/2NOGHLb.

Addenda

[1] Don Braid, "Notley Government in a Headlong Rush," *Calgary Herald*, November 3, 2016, A4.

[2] Co-operative Commonwealth Federation, The Regina Manifesto, 1993, https://bit.ly/1pu3QLR.

[3] New Democratic Party (Alberta), Constitution, Appendix C, June 2016.

[4] Terence Corcoran, "Jack Layton's Hidden Agenda," *National Post*, April 30, 2011, FP18.

[5] Thomas Sowell, *Knowledge and Decisions* (New York: Basic Books: 1986), 12.

[6] Margaret Thatcher, Interview for *Woman's Own*, September 23, 1987, https://bit.ly/2l1r7yV.

[7] Max Roser and Esteban Ortiz-Ospina, "Global Extreme Poverty," *OurWorldInData.org*, March 27, 2017, https://bit.ly/2FvAe3E.

[8] Amnesty International, Annual Report: Venezuela, 2010, https://bit.ly/2O3OYe2.

[9] Thomas Lukaszuk, Twitter, 9:02 a.m., May 3, 2015, https://bit.ly/2N9a2Q4.

[10] Pascal Fontaine, "Communism in Latin America," in Stéphane Courtois, Nicolas Werth, Jean-Louis Panné, Andrezej Paczkowski, Karel Bartošek, and Jean Louis Margolin, translated by Jonathan Murphy and Mark Kramer, *The Black Book of Communism: Crimes, Terror, Repression* (Cambridge, Massachusetts: Harvard University Press, 1999), 651–654.

[11] Andrew Annandale Sinclair, "Che Guevara," *Encyclopaedia Brittanica*, undated, https://bit.ly/2wC5nM3\.

[12] Pascal Fontaine.

[13] Pascal Fontaine, 651.

[14] Jason Markusoff, "The Notley Cabinet: Where Her Top Talent Will Come From," *Calgary Herald,* May 7, 2015, https://bit.ly/2MNrV7P.

[15] Damien McElroy, "Chavez Pushes Venezuela Into Food War," *Daily Telegraph*, June 23, 2010, https://bit.ly/2vrPPKe.

[16] Ibid.

[17] TML Daily, "Venezuelan People Show Their Mettle," March 7, 2013, https://bit.ly/2Ccy7RN.

[18] Mark Wierzbicki, "NDP Leadership Candidates Tour Stops In Leduc," *Leduc Representative*, September 19, 2014, 6.

[19] Barry Cooper and Mebs Kanji, *Governing in Post-Deficit Times: Alberta in the Klein Years* (Calgary: University of Calgary, 2000), 73.

[20] Mark Lisac, *The Klein Revolution* (Edmonton: NeWest Press, 2005), 236.

[21] Kevin Taft, *Shredding the Public Interest: Ralph Klein and 25 Years of One-Party Government* (Edmonton: University of Alberta Press/Parkland Institute, 1997), 104.

[22] Ibid., 109–110.

[23] Ibid., 19.

[24] Frank Dabbs, *Ralph Klein: A Maverick Life* (Vancouver: Greystone Books,1995), xi.

[25] Ibid., 177.

[26] Don Martin, *King Ralph, The Political Life and Success of Ralph Klein* (Toronto: Key Porter Books, 142).

[27] Ibid., 157.

[28] Barry Cooper and Mebs Kanji, G*overning in Post-Deficit Times: Alberta in the Klein Years* (Calgary: University of Calgary, 2000), 1.

Index

Additional copies of *Ralph vs. Rachel*

Volume discounts for *Ralph vs. Rachel* are available by contacting the author directly though his website at **www.markmilke.com** or **mark@markmilke.com**.